RUNNING QUOTES

ULTIMATE
DAILY LOGBOOK

FARTLEK RUNNING PRESS
KANSAS CITY
ALL RIGHTS RESERVED
COPYRIGHT©2019

"I WOULD RATHER BE ASHES THAN DUST!

I WOULD RATHER THAT MY SPARK SHOULD
    BURN OUT IN A BRILLIANT BLAZE
    THAN IT SHOULD BE STIFLED BY DRY-ROT.

I WOULD RATHER BE A SUPERB METEOR,
    EVERY ATOM OF ME IN MAGNIFICENT GLOW,
    THAN A SLEEPY AND PERMANENT PLANET.

THE FUNCTION OF MAN IS TO LIVE, NOT TO EXIST.

I SHALL NOT WASTE MY DAYS
    TRYING TO PROLONG THEM.

    I SHALL USE MY TIME."

— JACK LONDON'S, 'CREDO'

THIS RUNNING QUOTES
ULTIMATE DAILY LOGBOOK
BELONGS TO:

NAME:_____

DATE:_____

PHONE:_____

EMAIL:_____

PACE CHART

TIME/ MILE	2 MILES	3.1 MILES 5 K	4 MILES	5 MILES	6.2 MILES 10 K	7.46 MILES 12 K
5:30	11:00	17:05	22:00	27:30	34:11	41:00
5:45	11:30	17:52	23:00	28:45	35:44	42:52
6:00	12:00	18:39	24:00	30:00	37:17	44:44
6:15	12:30	19:25	25:00	31:15	38:50	46:36
6:30	13:00	20:12	26:00	32:30	40:23	48:28
6:45	13:30	20:58	27:00	33:45	41:57	50:20
7:00	14:00	21:45	28:00	35:00	43:30	52:12
7:15	14:30	22:32	29:00	36:15	45:03	54:03
7:30	15:00	23:18	30:00	37:30	46:36	55:55
7:45	15:30	24:05	31:00	38:45	48:10	57:47
8:00	16:00	24:51	32:00	40:00	49:43	59:39
8:15	16:30	25:38	33:00	41:15	51:16	1:01:31
8:30	17:00	26:25	34:00	42:30	52:49	1:03:23
8:45	17:30	27:11	35:00	43:45	54:22	1:05:14
9:00	18:00	27:58	36:00	45:00	55:56	1:07:06
9:15	18:30	28:44	37:00	46:15	57:29	1:08:58
9:30	19:00	29:31	38:00	47:30	59:02	1:10:50
9:45	19:30	30:18	39:00	48:45	1:00:35	1:12:42
10:00	20:00	31:04	40:00	50:00	1:02:08	1:14:34
10:30	21:00	32:37	42:00	52:30	1:05:15	1:18:17
11:00	22:00	34:11	44:00	55:00	1:08:21	1:22:01
11:30	23:00	35:44	46:00	57:30	1:11:28	1:25:45
12:00	24:00	37:17	48:00	1:00:00	1:14:34	1:29:28
12:30	25:00	38:50	50:00	1:02:30	1:17:41	1:33:12
13:00	26:00	40:23	52:00	1:05:00	1:20:47	1:36:56
13:30	27:00	41:57	54:00	1:07:30	1:23:53	1:40:39
14:00	28:00	43:30	56:00	1:10:00	1:27:00	1:44:23

PACE CHART

9.3 MILES 15 K	10 MILES	12.43 MILES 20 K	13.1 MILES 1/2 MARA	15 MILES	20 MILES	26.2 MILES MARATHON
51:16	55:00	1:08:21	1:12:06	1:22:30	1:50:00	2:24:12
53:36	57:30	1:11:27	1:15:23	1:26:15	1:55:00	2;30:46
56:56	1:00:00	1:14:34	1:18:39	1:30:00	2:00:00	2:37:19
58:15	1:02:30	1:17:40	1:21:56	1:33:45	2:05:00	2:43:52
1:00:35	1:05:00	1:20:47	1:25:13	1:37:30	2:10:00	2:50:25
1:02:55	1:07:30	1:23:53	1:28:29	1:41:15	2:15:00	2:56:59
1:05:15	1:10:00	1:26:59	1:31:46	1:45:00	2:20:00	3:03:32
1:07:35	1:12:30	1:30:06	1:35:02	1:48:45	2:25:00	3:10:05
1:09:54	1:15:00	1:33:12	1:38:19	1:52:30	2:30:00	3:16:39
1:12:14	1:17:30	1:36:19	1:41:36	1:56:15	2:35:00	3:23:12
1:14:34	1:20:00	1:39:25	1:44:52	2:00:00	2:40:00	3:29:45
1:16:54	1:22:30	1:42:31	1:48:09	2:03:45	2:45:00	3:36:18
1:19:14	1:25:00	1:45:38	1:51:26	2:07:30	2:50:00	3:42:52
1:21:34	1:27:30	1:48:44	1:54:42	2:11:15	2:55:00	3:49:25
1:23:53	1:30:00	1:51:51	1:57:59	2:15:00	3:00:00	3:55:58
1:26:13	1:32:30	1:54:57	2:01:15	2:18:45	3:05:00	4:02:32
1:28:33	1:35:00	1:58:03	2:04:32	2:22:30	3:10:00	4:09:05
1:30:53	1:37:30	2:01:10	2:07:49	2:26:15	3:15:00	4:15:38
1:33:13	1:40:00	2:04:16	2:11:05	2:30:00	3:20:00	4:22:11
1:37:52	1:45:00	2:10:29	2:17:39	2:37:30	3:30:00	4:35:18
1:42:32	1:50:00	2:26:42	2:24:12	2:45:00	3:40:00	4:48:25
1:47:11	1:55:00	2:22:55	2:30:45	2:52:30	3:50:00	5:01:31
1:51:51	2:00:00	2:29:07	2:37:18	3:00:00	4:00:00	5:15:37
1:56:31	2:05:00	2:35:20	2:43:52	3:07:30	4:10:00	5:27:44
2:01:10	2:10:00	2:41:33	2:50:25	3:15:00	4:20:00	5:40:51
2:05:50	2:15:00	2:47:46	2:56:58	3:22:30	4:30:00	5:53:57
2:10:30	2:20:00	2:53:59	3:03:32	3:30:00	4;40:00	6:07:04

2019 2020 2021

2019

January
S	M	T	W	T	F	S
		1	2	3	4	5
6	7	8	9	10	11	12
13	14	15	16	17	18	19
20	21	22	23	24	25	26
27	28	29	30	31		

February
S	M	T	W	T	F	S
					1	2
3	4	5	6	7	8	9
10	11	12	13	14	15	16
17	18	19	20	21	22	23
24	25	26	27	28		

March
S	M	T	W	T	F	S
31					1	2
3	4	5	6	7	8	9
10	11	12	13	14	15	16
17	18	19	20	21	22	23
24	25	26	27	28	29	30

April
S	M	T	W	T	F	S
	1	2	3	4	5	6
7	8	9	10	11	12	13
14	15	16	17	18	19	20
21	22	23	24	25	26	27
28	29	30				

May
S	M	T	W	T	F	S
			1	2	3	4
5	6	7	8	9	10	11
12	13	14	15	16	17	18
19	20	21	22	23	24	25
26	27	28	29	30	31	

June
S	M	T	W	T	F	S
30						1
2	3	4	5	6	7	8
9	10	11	12	13	14	15
16	17	18	19	20	21	22
23	24	25	26	27	28	29

July
S	M	T	W	T	F	S
	1	2	3	4	5	6
7	8	9	10	11	12	13
14	15	16	17	18	19	20
21	22	23	24	25	26	27
28	29	30	31			

August
S	M	T	W	T	F	S
				1	2	3
4	5	6	7	8	9	10
11	12	13	14	15	16	17
18	19	20	21	22	23	24
25	26	27	28	29	30	31

September
S	M	T	W	T	F	S
1	2	3	4	5	6	7
8	9	10	11	12	13	14
15	16	17	18	19	20	21
22	23	24	25	26	27	28
29	30					

October
S	M	T	W	T	F	S
		1	2	3	4	5
6	7	8	9	10	11	12
13	14	15	16	17	18	19
20	21	22	23	24	25	26
27	28	29	30	31		

November
S	M	T	W	T	F	S
					1	2
3	4	5	6	7	8	9
10	11	12	13	14	15	16
17	18	19	20	21	22	23
24	25	26	27	28	29	30

December
S	M	T	W	T	F	S
1	2	3	4	5	6	7
8	9	10	11	12	13	14
15	16	17	18	19	20	21
22	23	24	25	26	27	28
29	30	31				

2020

January
S	M	T	W	T	F	S
			1	2	3	4
5	6	7	8	9	10	11
12	13	14	15	16	17	18
19	20	21	22	23	24	25
26	27	28	29	30	31	

February
S	M	T	W	T	F	S
						1
2	3	4	5	6	7	8
9	10	11	12	13	14	15
16	17	18	19	20	21	22
23	24	25	26	27	28	29

March
S	M	T	W	T	F	S
1	2	3	4	5	6	7
8	9	10	11	12	13	14
15	16	17	18	19	20	21
22	23	24	25	26	27	28
29	30	31				

April
S	M	T	W	T	F	S
			1	2	3	4
5	6	7	8	9	10	11
12	13	14	15	16	17	18
19	20	21	22	23	24	25
26	27	28	29	30		

May
S	M	T	W	T	F	S
31					1	2
3	4	5	6	7	8	9
10	11	12	13	14	15	16
17	18	19	20	21	22	23
24	25	26	27	28	29	30

June
S	M	T	W	T	F	S
	1	2	3	4	5	6
7	8	9	10	11	12	13
14	15	16	17	18	19	20
21	22	23	24	25	26	27
28	29	30				

July
S	M	T	W	T	F	S
			1	2	3	4
5	6	7	8	9	10	11
12	13	14	15	16	17	18
19	20	21	22	23	24	25
26	27	28	29	30	31	

August
S	M	T	W	T	F	S
30	31					1
2	3	4	5	6	7	8
9	10	11	12	13	14	15
16	17	18	19	20	21	22
23	24	25	26	27	28	29

September
S	M	T	W	T	F	S
		1	2	3	4	5
6	7	8	9	10	11	12
13	14	15	16	17	18	19
20	21	22	23	24	25	26
27	28	29	30			

October
S	M	T	W	T	F	S
				1	2	3
4	5	6	7	8	9	10
11	12	13	14	15	16	17
18	19	20	21	22	23	24
25	26	27	28	29	30	31

November
S	M	T	W	T	F	S
1	2	3	4	5	6	7
8	9	10	11	12	13	14
15	16	17	18	19	20	21
22	23	24	25	26	27	28
29	30					

December
S	M	T	W	T	F	S
		1	2	3	4	5
6	7	8	9	10	11	12
13	14	15	16	17	18	19
20	21	22	23	24	25	26
27	28	29	30	31		

2021

January
S	M	T	W	T	F	S
31					1	2
3	4	5	6	7	8	9
10	11	12	13	14	15	16
17	18	19	20	21	22	23
24	25	26	27	28	29	30

February
S	M	T	W	T	F	S
	1	2	3	4	5	6
7	8	9	10	11	12	13
14	15	16	17	18	19	20
21	22	23	24	25	26	27
28						

March
S	M	T	W	T	F	S
	1	2	3	4	5	6
7	8	9	10	11	12	13
14	15	16	17	18	19	20
21	22	23	24	25	26	27
28	29	30	31			

April
S	M	T	W	T	F	S
				1	2	3
4	5	6	7	8	9	10
11	12	13	14	15	16	17
18	19	20	21	22	23	24
25	26	27	28	29	30	

May
S	M	T	W	T	F	S
30	31					1
2	3	4	5	6	7	8
9	10	11	12	13	14	15
16	17	18	19	20	21	22
23	24	25	26	27	28	29

June
S	M	T	W	T	F	S
		1	2	3	4	5
6	7	8	9	10	11	12
13	14	15	16	17	18	19
20	21	22	23	24	25	26
27	28	29	30			

July
S	M	T	W	T	F	S
				1	2	3
4	5	6	7	8	9	10
11	12	13	14	15	16	17
18	19	20	21	22	23	24
25	26	27	28	29	30	31

August
S	M	T	W	T	F	S
1	2	3	4	5	6	7
8	9	10	11	12	13	14
15	16	17	18	19	20	21
22	23	24	25	26	27	28
29	30	31				

September
S	M	T	W	T	F	S
			1	2	3	4
5	6	7	8	9	10	11
12	13	14	15	16	17	18
19	20	21	22	23	24	25
26	27	28	29	30		

October
S	M	T	W	T	F	S
31					1	2
3	4	5	6	7	8	9
10	11	12	13	14	15	16
17	18	19	20	21	22	23
24	25	26	27	28	29	30

November
S	M	T	W	T	F	S
	1	2	3	4	5	6
7	8	9	10	11	12	13
14	15	16	17	18	19	20
21	22	23	24	25	26	27
28	29	30				

December
S	M	T	W	T	F	S
			1	2	3	4
5	6	7	8	9	10	11
12	13	14	15	16	17	18
19	20	21	22	23	24	25
26	27	28	29	30	31	

2022 2023 2024

2022

January
S	M	T	W	T	F	S
30	31					1
2	3	4	5	6	7	8
9	10	11	12	13	14	15
16	17	18	19	20	21	22
23	24	25	26	27	28	29

February
S	M	T	W	T	F	S
		1	2	3	4	5
6	7	8	9	10	11	12
13	14	15	16	17	18	19
20	21	22	23	24	25	26
27	28					

March
S	M	T	W	T	F	S
		1	2	3	4	5
6	7	8	9	10	11	12
13	14	15	16	17	18	19
20	21	22	23	24	25	26
27	28	29	30	31		

April
S	M	T	W	T	F	S
					1	2
3	4	5	6	7	8	9
10	11	12	13	14	15	16
17	18	19	20	21	22	23
24	25	26	27	28	29	30

May
S	M	T	W	T	F	S
1	2	3	4	5	6	7
8	9	10	11	12	13	14
15	16	17	18	19	20	21
22	23	24	25	26	27	28
29	30	31				

June
S	M	T	W	T	F	S
			1	2	3	4
5	6	7	8	9	10	11
12	13	14	15	16	17	18
19	20	21	22	23	24	25
26	27	28	29	30		

July
S	M	T	W	T	F	S
31					1	2
3	4	5	6	7	8	9
10	11	12	13	14	15	16
17	18	19	20	21	22	23
24	25	26	27	28	29	30

August
S	M	T	W	T	F	S
	1	2	3	4	5	6
7	8	9	10	11	12	13
14	15	16	17	18	19	20
21	22	23	24	25	26	27
28	29	30	31			

September
S	M	T	W	T	F	S
				1	2	3
4	5	6	7	8	9	10
11	12	13	14	15	16	17
18	19	20	21	22	23	24
25	26	27	28	29	30	

October
S	M	T	W	T	F	S
30	31					1
2	3	4	5	6	7	8
9	10	11	12	13	14	15
16	17	18	19	20	21	22
23	24	25	26	27	28	29

November
S	M	T	W	T	F	S
		1	2	3	4	5
6	7	8	9	10	11	12
13	14	15	16	17	18	19
20	21	22	23	24	25	26
27	28	29	30			

December
S	M	T	W	T	F	S
				1	2	3
4	5	6	7	8	9	10
11	12	13	14	15	16	17
18	19	20	21	22	23	24
25	26	27	28	29	30	31

2023

January
S	M	T	W	T	F	S
1	2	3	4	5	6	7
8	9	10	11	12	13	14
15	16	17	18	19	20	21
22	23	24	25	26	27	28
29	30	31				

February
S	M	T	W	T	F	S
			1	2	3	4
5	6	7	8	9	10	11
12	13	14	15	16	17	18
19	20	21	22	23	24	25
26	27	28				

March
S	M	T	W	T	F	S
			1	2	3	4
5	6	7	8	9	10	11
12	13	14	15	16	17	18
19	20	21	22	23	24	25
26	27	28	29	30	31	

April
S	M	T	W	T	F	S
30						1
2	3	4	5	6	7	8
9	10	11	12	13	14	15
16	17	18	19	20	21	22
23	24	25	26	27	28	29

May
S	M	T	W	T	F	S
	1	2	3	4	5	6
7	8	9	10	11	12	13
14	15	16	17	18	19	20
21	22	23	24	25	26	27
28	29	30	31			

June
S	M	T	W	T	F	S
				1	2	3
4	5	6	7	8	9	10
11	12	13	14	15	16	17
18	19	20	21	22	23	24
25	26	27	28	29	30	

July
S	M	T	W	T	F	S
30	31					1
2	3	4	5	6	7	8
9	10	11	12	13	14	15
16	17	18	19	20	21	22
23	24	25	26	27	28	29

August
S	M	T	W	T	F	S
		1	2	3	4	5
6	7	8	9	10	11	12
13	14	15	16	17	18	19
20	21	22	23	24	25	26
27	28	29	30	31		

September
S	M	T	W	T	F	S
					1	2
3	4	5	6	7	8	9
10	11	12	13	14	15	16
17	18	19	20	21	22	23
24	25	26	27	28	29	30

October
S	M	T	W	T	F	S
1	2	3	4	5	6	7
8	9	10	11	12	13	14
15	16	17	18	19	20	21
22	23	24	25	26	27	28
29	30	31				

November
S	M	T	W	T	F	S
31			1	2	3	4
5	6	7	8	9	10	11
12	13	14	15	16	17	18
19	20	21	22	23	24	25
26	27	28	29	30		

December
S	M	T	W	T	F	S
					1	2
3	4	5	6	7	8	9
10	11	12	13	14	15	16
17	18	19	20	21	22	23
24	25	26	27	28	29	30
31						

2024

January
S	M	T	W	T	F	S
	1	2	3	4	5	6
7	8	9	10	11	12	13
14	15	16	17	18	19	20
21	22	23	24	25	26	27
28	29	30	31			

February
S	M	T	W	T	F	S
				1	2	3
4	5	6	7	8	9	10
11	12	13	14	15	16	17
18	19	20	21	22	23	24
25	26	27	28	29		

March
S	M	T	W	T	F	S
31					1	2
3	4	5	6	7	8	9
10	11	12	13	14	15	16
17	18	19	20	21	22	23
24	25	26	27	28	29	30

April
S	M	T	W	T	F	S
	1	2	3	4	5	6
7	8	9	10	11	12	13
14	15	16	17	18	19	20
21	22	23	24	25	26	27
28	29	30				

May
S	M	T	W	T	F	S
			1	2	3	4
5	6	7	8	9	10	11
12	13	14	15	16	17	18
19	20	21	22	23	24	25
26	27	28	29	30	31	

June
S	M	T	W	T	F	S
30						1
2	3	4	5	6	7	8
9	10	11	12	13	14	15
16	17	18	19	20	21	22
23	24	25	26	27	28	29

July
S	M	T	W	T	F	S
	1	2	3	4	5	6
7	8	9	10	11	12	13
14	15	16	17	18	19	20
21	22	23	24	25	26	27
28	29	30	31			

August
S	M	T	W	T	F	S
				1	2	3
4	5	6	7	8	9	10
11	12	13	14	15	16	17
18	19	20	21	22	23	24
25	26	27	28	29	30	31

September
S	M	T	W	T	F	S
1	2	3	4	5	6	7
8	9	10	11	12	13	14
15	16	17	18	19	20	21
22	23	24	25	26	27	28
29	30					

October
S	M	T	W	T	F	S
		1	2	3	4	5
6	7	8	9	10	11	12
13	14	15	16	17	18	19
20	21	22	23	24	25	26
27	28	29	30	31		

November
S	M	T	W	T	F	S
					1	2
3	4	5	6	7	8	9
10	11	12	13	14	15	16
17	18	19	20	21	22	23
24	25	26	27	28	29	30

December
S	M	T	W	T	F	S
1	2	3	4	5	6	7
8	9	10	11	12	13	14
15	16	17	18	19	20	21
22	23	24	25	26	27	28
29	30	31				

A YEAR'S WORTH OF MILES

	JAN	FEB	MARCH	APRIL	MAY	JUNE
1						
2						
3						
4						
5						
6						
7						
8						
9						
10						
11						
12						
13						
14						
15						
16						
17						
18						
19						
20						
21						
22						
23						
24						
25						
26						
27						
28						
29						
30						
31						

AT A GLANCE — YEAR:

	JULY	AUG	SEPT	OCT	NOV	DEC
1						
2						
3						
4						
5						
6						
7						
8						
9						
10						
11						
12						
13						
14						
15						
16						
17						
18						
19						
20						
21						
22						
23						
24						
25						
26						
27						
28						
29						
30						
31						

RACING RESULTS

#	DATE	RACE NAME/ LOCATION	DISTANCE	TIME/ PACE	PLACE/ FIELD	ROAD, TRACK, ETC

RACING RESULTS

#	DATE	RACE NAME/ LOCATION	DISTANCE	TIME/ PACE	PLACE/ FIELD	ROAD, TRACK, ETC

PROGRESS OF PERSONAL BESTS

400 METER

800 METER

1500 METER

1 MILE

PROGRESS OF PERSONAL BESTS

5 K

10 K

1/2 MARATHON

MARATHON

HEART RATE & WEIGHT
3 MONTHS AT A GLANCE

	WEIGHT	HR	WEIGHT	HR	WEIGHT	HR
1						
2						
3						
4						
5						
6						
7						
8						
9						
10						
11						
12						
13						
14						
15						
16						
17						
18						
19						
20						
21						
22						
23						
24						
25						
26						
27						
28						
29						
30						
31						

HEART RATE & WEIGHT
3 MONTHS AT A GLANCE

	WEIGHT	HR	WEIGHT	HR	WEIGHT	HR
1						
2						
3						
4						
5						
6						
7						
8						
9						
10						
11						
12						
13						
14						
15						
16						
17						
18						
19						
20						
21						
22						
23						
24						
25						
26						
27						
28						
29						
30						
31						

HEART RATE & WEIGHT
3 MONTHS AT A GLANCE

	WEIGHT	HR	WEIGHT	HR	WEIGHT	HR
1						
2						
3						
4						
5						
6						
7						
8						
9						
10						
11						
12						
13						
14						
15						
16						
17						
18						
19						
20						
21						
22						
23						
24						
25						
26						
27						
28						
29						
30						
31						

HEART RATE & WEIGHT
3 MONTHS AT A GLANCE

	WEIGHT	HR	WEIGHT	HR	WEIGHT	HR
1						
2						
3						
4						
5						
6						
7						
8						
9						
10						
11						
12						
13						
14						
15						
16						
17						
18						
19						
20						
21						
22						
23						
24						
25						
26						
27						
28						
29						
30						
31						

MONTH OF:

MON	TUES	WED	THURS
I DO NOT LIVE FOR WHAT THE WORLD THINKS OF ME, BUT FOR WHAT I THINK OF MYSELF. — JACK LONDON			

NOTES:

YEAR OF:

FRI	SAT	SUN	MONTHLY MUST DO LIST

MONTHLY GOALS

AFFIRMATIONS:

MONTH: _____ WEEK OF: _____

GOALS: _____

_____

YOUR
FAVORITE
QUOTE
FOR THE WEEK:

MONDAY:		
TIME:	PACE:	AVG. HEART RATE:
TODAY'S DISTANCE:		WEATHER/TEMP:
TOTAL DISTANCE:		MOOD ☺ ☺ ☹

TUESDAY:		
TIME:	PACE:	AVG. HEART RATE:
TODAY'S DISTANCE:		WEATHER/TEMP:
TOTAL DISTANCE:		MOOD ☺ ☺ ☹

WEDNESDAY:		
TIME:	PACE:	AVG. HEART RATE:
TODAY'S DISTANCE:		WEATHER/TEMP:
TOTAL DISTANCE:		MOOD ☺ ☺ ☹

THURSDAY:		
TIME:	PACE:	AVG. HEART RATE:
TODAY'S DISTANCE:		WEATHER/TEMP:
TOTAL DISTANCE:		MOOD ☺ ☺ ☹

FRIDAY:

TIME: PACE: AVG. HEART RATE:

TODAY'S DISTANCE: WEATHER/TEMP:

TOTAL DISTANCE: MOOD ☺ 😐 ☹

SATURDAY:

TIME: PACE: AVG. HEART RATE:

TODAY'S DISTANCE: WEATHER/TEMP:

TOTAL DISTANCE: MOOD ☺ 😐 ☹

SUNDAY:

TIME: PACE: AVG. HEART RATE:

TODAY'S DISTANCE: WEATHER/TEMP:

TOTAL DISTANCE: MOOD ☺ 😐 ☹

WEEKLY SUMMARY & OBSERVATIONS:

SHORTEST RUN: LONGEST RUN: AVERAGE RUN:

WEEK TOTAL: MONTH TOTAL: YEAR TO DATE:

	M	T	W	TH	F	SA	SU
WEIGHT							
AM PULSE							
GLUCOSE							
KETONES BLOOD OR URINE							

MONTH: _____ WEEK OF: _____

GOALS: _____

_____

YOUR
FAVORITE
QUOTE
FOR THE WEEK:

MONDAY:		
TIME:	PACE:	AVG. HEART RATE:
TODAY'S DISTANCE:		WEATHER/TEMP:
TOTAL DISTANCE:		MOOD ☺ 😐 ☹

TUESDAY:		
TIME:	PACE:	AVG. HEART RATE:
TODAY'S DISTANCE:		WEATHER/TEMP:
TOTAL DISTANCE:		MOOD ☺ 😐 ☹

WEDNESDAY:		
TIME:	PACE:	AVG. HEART RATE:
TODAY'S DISTANCE:		WEATHER/TEMP:
TOTAL DISTANCE:		MOOD ☺ 😐 ☹

THURSDAY:		
TIME:	PACE:	AVG. HEART RATE:
TODAY'S DISTANCE:		WEATHER/TEMP:
TOTAL DISTANCE:		MOOD ☺ 😐 ☹

FRIDAY:

TIME: PACE: AVG. HEART RATE:

TODAY'S DISTANCE: WEATHER/TEMP:

TOTAL DISTANCE: MOOD ☺ 😐 ☹

SATURDAY:

TIME: PACE: AVG. HEART RATE:

TODAY'S DISTANCE: WEATHER/TEMP:

TOTAL DISTANCE: MOOD ☺ 😐 ☹

SUNDAY:

TIME: PACE: AVG. HEART RATE:

TODAY'S DISTANCE: WEATHER/TEMP:

TOTAL DISTANCE: MOOD ☺ 😐 ☹

WEEKLY SUMMARY & OBSERVATIONS:

SHORTEST RUN: LONGEST RUN: AVERAGE RUN:

WEEK TOTAL: MONTH TOTAL: YEAR TO DATE:

	M	T	W	TH	F	SA	SU
WEIGHT							
AM PULSE							
GLUCOSE							
KETONES BLOOD OR URINE							

MONTH: _____ WEEK OF: _____

GOALS: _____
_____

YOUR
FAVORITE
QUOTE
FOR THE WEEK:

MONDAY:

TIME: PACE: AVG. HEART RATE:

TODAY'S DISTANCE: WEATHER/TEMP:

TOTAL DISTANCE: MOOD ☺   😐   ☹

TUESDAY:

TIME: PACE: AVG. HEART RATE:

TODAY'S DISTANCE: WEATHER/TEMP:

TOTAL DISTANCE: MOOD ☺   😐   ☹

WEDNESDAY:

TIME: PACE: AVG. HEART RATE:

TODAY'S DISTANCE: WEATHER/TEMP:

TOTAL DISTANCE: MOOD ☺   😐   ☹

THURSDAY:

TIME: PACE: AVG. HEART RATE:

TODAY'S DISTANCE: WEATHER/TEMP:

TOTAL DISTANCE: MOOD ☺   😐   ☹

FRIDAY:

TIME: PACE: AVG. HEART RATE:

TODAY'S DISTANCE: WEATHER/TEMP:

TOTAL DISTANCE: MOOD ☺ 😐 ☹

SATURDAY:

TIME: PACE: AVG. HEART RATE:

TODAY'S DISTANCE: WEATHER/TEMP:

TOTAL DISTANCE: MOOD ☺ 😐 ☹

SUNDAY:

TIME: PACE: AVG. HEART RATE:

TODAY'S DISTANCE: WEATHER/TEMP:

TOTAL DISTANCE: MOOD ☺ 😐 ☹

WEEKLY SUMMARY & OBSERVATIONS:

SHORTEST RUN: LONGEST RUN: AVERAGE RUN:

WEEK TOTAL: MONTH TOTAL: YEAR TO DATE:

	M	T	W	TH	F	SA	SU
WEIGHT							
AM PULSE							
GLUCOSE							
KETONES BLOOD OR URINE							

MONTH: _____ WEEK OF: _____

GOALS: _____
_____

YOUR
FAVORITE
QUOTE
FOR THE WEEK:

MONDAY:

TIME: PACE: AVG. HEART RATE:

TODAY'S DISTANCE: WEATHER/TEMP:

TOTAL DISTANCE: MOOD ☺ 😐 ☹

TUESDAY:

TIME: PACE: AVG. HEART RATE:

TODAY'S DISTANCE: WEATHER/TEMP:

TOTAL DISTANCE: MOOD ☺ 😐 ☹

WEDNESDAY:

TIME: PACE: AVG. HEART RATE:

TODAY'S DISTANCE: WEATHER/TEMP:

TOTAL DISTANCE: MOOD ☺ 😐 ☹

THURSDAY:

TIME: PACE: AVG. HEART RATE:

TODAY'S DISTANCE: WEATHER/TEMP:

TOTAL DISTANCE: MOOD ☺ 😐 ☹

FRIDAY:

TIME: PACE: AVG. HEART RATE:

TODAY'S DISTANCE: WEATHER/TEMP:

TOTAL DISTANCE: MOOD ☺ 😐 ☹

SATURDAY:

TIME: PACE: AVG. HEART RATE:

TODAY'S DISTANCE: WEATHER/TEMP:

TOTAL DISTANCE: MOOD ☺ 😐 ☹

SUNDAY:

TIME: PACE: AVG. HEART RATE:

TODAY'S DISTANCE: WEATHER/TEMP:

TOTAL DISTANCE: MOOD ☺ 😐 ☹

WEEKLY SUMMARY & OBSERVATIONS:

SHORTEST RUN: LONGEST RUN: AVERAGE RUN:

WEEK TOTAL: MONTH TOTAL: YEAR TO DATE:

	M	T	W	TH	F	SA	SU
WEIGHT							
AM PULSE							
GLUCOSE							
KETONES BLOOD OR URINE							

MONTH: _____   WEEK OF: _____

GOALS: _____

_____

YOUR
FAVORITE
QUOTE
FOR THE WEEK:

MONDAY:		
TIME: PACE:	AVG. HEART RATE:	
TODAY'S DISTANCE:	WEATHER/TEMP:	
TOTAL DISTANCE:	MOOD ☺ ☺ ☹	

TUESDAY:		
TIME: PACE:	AVG. HEART RATE:	
TODAY'S DISTANCE:	WEATHER/TEMP:	
TOTAL DISTANCE:	MOOD ☺ ☺ ☹	

WEDNESDAY:		
TIME: PACE:	AVG. HEART RATE:	
TODAY'S DISTANCE:	WEATHER/TEMP:	
TOTAL DISTANCE:	MOOD ☺ ☺ ☹	

THURSDAY:		
TIME: PACE:	AVG. HEART RATE:	
TODAY'S DISTANCE:	WEATHER/TEMP:	
TOTAL DISTANCE:	MOOD ☺ ☺ ☹	

FRIDAY:

TIME: PACE: AVG. HEART RATE:

TODAY'S DISTANCE: WEATHER/TEMP:

TOTAL DISTANCE: MOOD ☺   😐   ☹

SATURDAY:

TIME: PACE: AVG. HEART RATE:

TODAY'S DISTANCE: WEATHER/TEMP:

TOTAL DISTANCE: MOOD ☺   😐   ☹

SUNDAY:

TIME: PACE: AVG. HEART RATE:

TODAY'S DISTANCE: WEATHER/TEMP:

TOTAL DISTANCE: MOOD ☺   😐   ☹

WEEKLY SUMMARY & OBSERVATIONS:

SHORTEST RUN: LONGEST RUN: AVERAGE RUN:

WEEK TOTAL: MONTH TOTAL: YEAR TO DATE:

	M	T	W	TH	F	SA	SU
WEIGHT							
AM PULSE							
GLUCOSE							
KETONES BLOOD OR URINE							

MONTH OF:

MON	TUES	WED	THURS
RUN LIKE YOU STOLE SOMETHING!			

NOTES:

YEAR OF:

FRI	SAT	SUN	MONTHLY MUST DO LIST

MONTHLY GOALS

AFFIRMATIONS:

MONTH: _____ WEEK OF: _____

GOALS: _____
_____

YOUR
FAVORITE
QUOTE
FOR THE WEEK:

MONDAY:		
TIME:	PACE:	AVG. HEART RATE:
TODAY'S DISTANCE:		WEATHER/TEMP:
TOTAL DISTANCE:		MOOD ☺ ☺ ☹

TUESDAY:		
TIME:	PACE:	AVG. HEART RATE:
TODAY'S DISTANCE:		WEATHER/TEMP:
TOTAL DISTANCE:		MOOD ☺ ☺ ☹

WEDNESDAY:		
TIME:	PACE:	AVG. HEART RATE:
TODAY'S DISTANCE:		WEATHER/TEMP:
TOTAL DISTANCE:		MOOD ☺ ☺ ☹

THURSDAY:		
TIME:	PACE:	AVG. HEART RATE:
TODAY'S DISTANCE:		WEATHER/TEMP:
TOTAL DISTANCE:		MOOD ☺ ☺ ☹

FRIDAY:

TIME: PACE: AVG. HEART RATE:

TODAY'S DISTANCE: WEATHER/TEMP:

TOTAL DISTANCE: MOOD ☺   😐   ☹

SATURDAY:

TIME: PACE: AVG. HEART RATE:

TODAY'S DISTANCE: WEATHER/TEMP:

TOTAL DISTANCE: MOOD ☺   😐   ☹

SUNDAY:

TIME: PACE: AVG. HEART RATE:

TODAY'S DISTANCE: WEATHER/TEMP:

TOTAL DISTANCE: MOOD ☺   😐   ☹

WEEKLY SUMMARY & OBSERVATIONS:

SHORTEST RUN: LONGEST RUN: AVERAGE RUN:

WEEK TOTAL: MONTH TOTAL: YEAR TO DATE:

	M	T	W	TH	F	SA	SU
WEIGHT							
AM PULSE							
GLUCOSE							
KETONES BLOOD OR URINE							

MONTH: _____   WEEK OF: _____

GOALS: _____
       _____

YOUR
FAVORITE
QUOTE
FOR THE WEEK:

MONDAY:		
TIME: PACE:	AVG. HEART RATE:	
TODAY'S DISTANCE:	WEATHER/TEMP:	
TOTAL DISTANCE:	MOOD ☺ 😐 ☹	

TUESDAY:		
TIME: PACE:	AVG. HEART RATE:	
TODAY'S DISTANCE:	WEATHER/TEMP:	
TOTAL DISTANCE:	MOOD ☺ 😐 ☹	

WEDNESDAY:		
TIME: PACE:	AVG. HEART RATE:	
TODAY'S DISTANCE:	WEATHER/TEMP:	
TOTAL DISTANCE:	MOOD ☺ 😐 ☹	

THURSDAY:		
TIME: PACE:	AVG. HEART RATE:	
TODAY'S DISTANCE:	WEATHER/TEMP:	
TOTAL DISTANCE:	MOOD ☺ 😐 ☹	

FRIDAY:

TIME: PACE: AVG. HEART RATE:

TODAY'S DISTANCE: WEATHER/TEMP:

TOTAL DISTANCE: MOOD ☺ 😐 ☹

SATURDAY:

TIME: PACE: AVG. HEART RATE:

TODAY'S DISTANCE: WEATHER/TEMP:

TOTAL DISTANCE: MOOD ☺ 😐 ☹

SUNDAY:

TIME: PACE: AVG. HEART RATE:

TODAY'S DISTANCE: WEATHER/TEMP:

TOTAL DISTANCE: MOOD ☺ 😐 ☹

WEEKLY SUMMARY & OBSERVATIONS:

SHORTEST RUN: LONGEST RUN: AVERAGE RUN:

WEEK TOTAL: MONTH TOTAL: YEAR TO DATE:

	M	T	W	TH	F	SA	SU
WEIGHT							
AM PULSE							
GLUCOSE							
KETONES BLOOD OR URINE							

MONTH: _____ WEEK OF: _____

GOALS: _____

_____

YOUR
FAVORITE
QUOTE
FOR THE WEEK:

MONDAY:		
TIME:	PACE:	AVG. HEART RATE:
TODAY'S DISTANCE:		WEATHER/TEMP:
TOTAL DISTANCE:		MOOD ☺ ☺ ☹

TUESDAY:		
TIME:	PACE:	AVG. HEART RATE:
TODAY'S DISTANCE:		WEATHER/TEMP:
TOTAL DISTANCE:		MOOD ☺ ☺ ☹

WEDNESDAY:		
TIME:	PACE:	AVG. HEART RATE:
TODAY'S DISTANCE:		WEATHER/TEMP:
TOTAL DISTANCE:		MOOD ☺ ☺ ☹

THURSDAY:		
TIME:	PACE:	AVG. HEART RATE:
TODAY'S DISTANCE:		WEATHER/TEMP:
TOTAL DISTANCE:		MOOD ☺ ☺ ☹

FRIDAY:

TIME: PACE: AVG. HEART RATE:

TODAY'S DISTANCE: WEATHER/TEMP:

TOTAL DISTANCE: MOOD ☺ 😐 ☹

SATURDAY:

TIME: PACE: AVG. HEART RATE:

TODAY'S DISTANCE: WEATHER/TEMP:

TOTAL DISTANCE: MOOD ☺ 😐 ☹

SUNDAY:

TIME: PACE: AVG. HEART RATE:

TODAY'S DISTANCE: WEATHER/TEMP:

TOTAL DISTANCE: MOOD ☺ 😐 ☹

WEEKLY SUMMARY & OBSERVATIONS:

SHORTEST RUN: LONGEST RUN: AVERAGE RUN:

WEEK TOTAL: MONTH TOTAL: YEAR TO DATE:

	M	T	W	TH	F	SA	SU
WEIGHT							
AM PULSE							
GLUCOSE							
KETONES BLOOD OR URINE							

MONTH: _____ WEEK OF: _____

GOALS: ....
....

YOUR
FAVORITE
QUOTE
FOR THE WEEK:

MONDAY:		
TIME:	PACE:	AVG. HEART RATE:
TODAY'S DISTANCE:		WEATHER/TEMP:
TOTAL DISTANCE:		MOOD ☺ 😐 ☹

TUESDAY:		
TIME:	PACE:	AVG. HEART RATE:
TODAY'S DISTANCE:		WEATHER/TEMP:
TOTAL DISTANCE:		MOOD ☺ 😐 ☹

WEDNESDAY:		
TIME:	PACE:	AVG. HEART RATE:
TODAY'S DISTANCE:		WEATHER/TEMP:
TOTAL DISTANCE:		MOOD ☺ 😐 ☹

THURSDAY:		
TIME:	PACE:	AVG. HEART RATE:
TODAY'S DISTANCE:		WEATHER/TEMP:
TOTAL DISTANCE:		MOOD ☺ 😐 ☹

FRIDAY:

TIME: PACE: AVG. HEART RATE:

TODAY'S DISTANCE: WEATHER/TEMP:

TOTAL DISTANCE: MOOD ☺ 😐 ☹

SATURDAY:

TIME: PACE: AVG. HEART RATE:

TODAY'S DISTANCE: WEATHER/TEMP:

TOTAL DISTANCE: MOOD ☺ 😐 ☹

SUNDAY:

TIME: PACE: AVG. HEART RATE:

TODAY'S DISTANCE: WEATHER/TEMP:

TOTAL DISTANCE: MOOD ☺ 😐 ☹

WEEKLY SUMMARY & OBSERVATIONS:

SHORTEST RUN: LONGEST RUN: AVERAGE RUN:

WEEK TOTAL: MONTH TOTAL: YEAR TO DATE:

	M	T	W	TH	F	SA	SU
WEIGHT							
AM PULSE							
GLUCOSE							
KETONES BLOOD OR URINE							

MONTH OF:

MON	TUES	WED	THURS
RUNNING IS MY THERAPY AND EVERY STEP I TAKE BRINGS ME JOY			

NOTES:

YEAR OF:

FRI	SAT	SUN

MONTHLY MUST DO LIST

_____
_____
_____
_____
_____
_____
_____
_____
_____

MONTHLY GOALS

_____
_____
_____
_____
_____
_____

AFFIRMATIONS:

MONTH: _____   WEEK OF: _____

GOALS: _____

_____

YOUR
FAVORITE
QUOTE
FOR THE WEEK:

MONDAY:		
TIME:	PACE:	AVG. HEART RATE:
TODAY'S DISTANCE:		WEATHER/TEMP:
TOTAL DISTANCE:		MOOD ☺ 😐 ☹

TUESDAY:		
TIME:	PACE:	AVG. HEART RATE:
TODAY'S DISTANCE:		WEATHER/TEMP:
TOTAL DISTANCE:		MOOD ☺ 😐 ☹

WEDNESDAY:		
TIME:	PACE:	AVG. HEART RATE:
TODAY'S DISTANCE:		WEATHER/TEMP:
TOTAL DISTANCE:		MOOD ☺ 😐 ☹

THURSDAY:		
TIME:	PACE:	AVG. HEART RATE:
TODAY'S DISTANCE:		WEATHER/TEMP:
TOTAL DISTANCE:		MOOD ☺ 😐 ☹

FRIDAY:

TIME: PACE: AVG. HEART RATE:

TODAY'S DISTANCE: WEATHER/TEMP:

TOTAL DISTANCE: MOOD ☺ 😐 ☹

SATURDAY:

TIME: PACE: AVG. HEART RATE:

TODAY'S DISTANCE: WEATHER/TEMP:

TOTAL DISTANCE: MOOD ☺ 😐 ☹

SUNDAY:

TIME: PACE: AVG. HEART RATE:

TODAY'S DISTANCE: WEATHER/TEMP:

TOTAL DISTANCE: MOOD ☺ 😐 ☹

WEEKLY SUMMARY & OBSERVATIONS:

SHORTEST RUN: LONGEST RUN: AVERAGE RUN:

WEEK TOTAL: MONTH TOTAL: YEAR TO DATE:

	M	T	W	TH	F	SA	SU
WEIGHT							
AM PULSE							
GLUCOSE							
KETONES BLOOD OR URINE							

MONTH: _____ WEEK OF: _____

GOALS: _____
_____

YOUR
FAVORITE
QUOTE
FOR THE WEEK:

MONDAY:

TIME: PACE: AVG. HEART RATE:

TODAY'S DISTANCE: WEATHER/TEMP:

TOTAL DISTANCE: MOOD ☺ 😐 ☹

TUESDAY:

TIME: PACE: AVG. HEART RATE:

TODAY'S DISTANCE: WEATHER/TEMP:

TOTAL DISTANCE: MOOD ☺ 😐 ☹

WEDNESDAY:

TIME: PACE: AVG. HEART RATE:

TODAY'S DISTANCE: WEATHER/TEMP:

TOTAL DISTANCE: MOOD ☺ 😐 ☹

THURSDAY:

TIME: PACE: AVG. HEART RATE:

TODAY'S DISTANCE: WEATHER/TEMP:

TOTAL DISTANCE: MOOD ☺ 😐 ☹

FRIDAY:

TIME: PACE: AVG. HEART RATE:

TODAY'S DISTANCE: WEATHER/TEMP:

TOTAL DISTANCE: MOOD ☺   😐   ☹

SATURDAY:

TIME: PACE: AVG. HEART RATE:

TODAY'S DISTANCE: WEATHER/TEMP:

TOTAL DISTANCE: MOOD ☺   😐   ☹

SUNDAY:

TIME: PACE: AVG. HEART RATE:

TODAY'S DISTANCE: WEATHER/TEMP:

TOTAL DISTANCE: MOOD ☺   😐   ☹

WEEKLY SUMMARY & OBSERVATIONS:

SHORTEST RUN: LONGEST RUN: AVERAGE RUN:

WEEK TOTAL: MONTH TOTAL: YEAR TO DATE:

	M	T	W	TH	F	SA	SU
WEIGHT							
AM PULSE							
GLUCOSE							
KETONES BLOOD OR URINE							

MONTH: _____ WEEK OF: _____

GOALS: _____

_____

YOUR
FAVORITE
QUOTE
FOR THE WEEK:

MONDAY:		
TIME:	PACE:	AVG. HEART RATE:
TODAY'S DISTANCE:		WEATHER/TEMP:
TOTAL DISTANCE:		MOOD ☺ ☺ ☹

TUESDAY:		
TIME:	PACE:	AVG. HEART RATE:
TODAY'S DISTANCE:		WEATHER/TEMP:
TOTAL DISTANCE:		MOOD ☺ ☺ ☹

WEDNESDAY:		
TIME:	PACE:	AVG. HEART RATE:
TODAY'S DISTANCE:		WEATHER/TEMP:
TOTAL DISTANCE:		MOOD ☺ ☺ ☹

THURSDAY:		
TIME:	PACE:	AVG. HEART RATE:
TODAY'S DISTANCE:		WEATHER/TEMP:
TOTAL DISTANCE:		MOOD ☺ ☺ ☹

FRIDAY:

TIME: PACE: AVG. HEART RATE:

TODAY'S DISTANCE: WEATHER/TEMP:

TOTAL DISTANCE: MOOD ☺   😐   ☹

SATURDAY:

TIME: PACE: AVG. HEART RATE:

TODAY'S DISTANCE: WEATHER/TEMP:

TOTAL DISTANCE: MOOD ☺   😐   ☹

SUNDAY:

TIME: PACE: AVG. HEART RATE:

TODAY'S DISTANCE: WEATHER/TEMP:

TOTAL DISTANCE: MOOD ☺   😐   ☹

WEEKLY SUMMARY & OBSERVATIONS:

SHORTEST RUN: LONGEST RUN: AVERAGE RUN:

WEEK TOTAL: MONTH TOTAL: YEAR TO DATE:

	M	T	W	TH	F	SA	SU
WEIGHT							
AM PULSE							
GLUCOSE							
KETONES BLOOD OR URINE							

MONTH: _____ **WEEK OF:** _____

GOALS: _____

_____

YOUR
FAVORITE
QUOTE
FOR THE WEEK:

MONDAY:

TIME: PACE: AVG. HEART RATE:

TODAY'S DISTANCE: WEATHER/TEMP:

TOTAL DISTANCE: MOOD ☺ 😐 ☹

TUESDAY:

TIME: PACE: AVG. HEART RATE:

TODAY'S DISTANCE: WEATHER/TEMP:

TOTAL DISTANCE: MOOD ☺ 😐 ☹

WEDNESDAY:

TIME: PACE: AVG. HEART RATE:

TODAY'S DISTANCE: WEATHER/TEMP:

TOTAL DISTANCE: MOOD ☺ 😐 ☹

THURSDAY:

TIME: PACE: AVG. HEART RATE:

TODAY'S DISTANCE: WEATHER/TEMP:

TOTAL DISTANCE: MOOD ☺ 😐 ☹

FRIDAY:

TIME: PACE: AVG. HEART RATE:

TODAY'S DISTANCE: WEATHER/TEMP:

TOTAL DISTANCE: MOOD ☺   😐   ☹

SATURDAY:

TIME: PACE: AVG. HEART RATE:

TODAY'S DISTANCE: WEATHER/TEMP:

TOTAL DISTANCE: MOOD ☺   😐   ☹

SUNDAY:

TIME: PACE: AVG. HEART RATE:

TODAY'S DISTANCE: WEATHER/TEMP:

TOTAL DISTANCE: MOOD ☺   😐   ☹

WEEKLY SUMMARY & OBSERVATIONS:

SHORTEST RUN: LONGEST RUN: AVERAGE RUN:

WEEK TOTAL: MONTH TOTAL: YEAR TO DATE:

	M	T	W	TH	F	SA	SU
WEIGHT							
AM PULSE							
GLUCOSE							
KETONES BLOOD OR URINE							

MONTH: _____ WEEK OF: _____

GOALS: _____

_____

YOUR
FAVORITE
QUOTE
FOR THE WEEK:

MONDAY:

TIME: PACE: AVG. HEART RATE:

TODAY'S DISTANCE: WEATHER/TEMP:

TOTAL DISTANCE: MOOD ☺ ☺ ☹

TUESDAY:

TIME: PACE: AVG. HEART RATE:

TODAY'S DISTANCE: WEATHER/TEMP:

TOTAL DISTANCE: MOOD ☺ ☺ ☹

WEDNESDAY:

TIME: PACE: AVG. HEART RATE:

TODAY'S DISTANCE: WEATHER/TEMP:

TOTAL DISTANCE: MOOD ☺ ☺ ☹

THURSDAY:

TIME: PACE: AVG. HEART RATE:

TODAY'S DISTANCE: WEATHER/TEMP:

TOTAL DISTANCE: MOOD ☺ ☺ ☹

FRIDAY:

TIME: PACE: AVG. HEART RATE:

TODAY'S DISTANCE: WEATHER/TEMP:

TOTAL DISTANCE: MOOD ☺   😐   ☹

SATURDAY:

TIME: PACE: AVG. HEART RATE:

TODAY'S DISTANCE: WEATHER/TEMP:

TOTAL DISTANCE: MOOD ☺   😐   ☹

SUNDAY:

TIME: PACE: AVG. HEART RATE:

TODAY'S DISTANCE: WEATHER/TEMP:

TOTAL DISTANCE: MOOD ☺   😐   ☹

WEEKLY SUMMARY & OBSERVATIONS:

SHORTEST RUN: LONGEST RUN: AVERAGE RUN:

WEEK TOTAL: MONTH TOTAL: YEAR TO DATE:

	M	T	W	TH	F	SA	SU
WEIGHT							
AM PULSE							
GLUCOSE							
KETONES BLOOD OR URINE							

MONTH OF:

MON	TUES	WED	THURS
RUN TO FIND YOUR INNER PEACE			

NOTES:

YEAR OF:

FRI	SAT	SUN	MONTHLY MUST DO LIST
			MONTHLY GOALS

AFFIRMATIONS:

MONTH: _____ WEEK OF: _____

GOALS: _____
_____

YOUR
FAVORITE
QUOTE
FOR THE WEEK:

MONDAY:

TIME: PACE: AVG. HEART RATE:

TODAY'S DISTANCE: WEATHER/TEMP:

TOTAL DISTANCE: MOOD ☺ 😐 ☹

TUESDAY:

TIME: PACE: AVG. HEART RATE:

TODAY'S DISTANCE: WEATHER/TEMP:

TOTAL DISTANCE: MOOD ☺ 😐 ☹

WEDNESDAY:

TIME: PACE: AVG. HEART RATE:

TODAY'S DISTANCE: WEATHER/TEMP:

TOTAL DISTANCE: MOOD ☺ 😐 ☹

THURSDAY:

TIME: PACE: AVG. HEART RATE:

TODAY'S DISTANCE: WEATHER/TEMP:

TOTAL DISTANCE: MOOD ☺ 😐 ☹

FRIDAY:

TIME: PACE: AVG. HEART RATE:

TODAY'S DISTANCE: WEATHER/TEMP:

TOTAL DISTANCE: MOOD ☺ 😐 ☹

SATURDAY:

TIME: PACE: AVG. HEART RATE:

TODAY'S DISTANCE: WEATHER/TEMP:

TOTAL DISTANCE: MOOD ☺ 😐 ☹

SUNDAY:

TIME: PACE: AVG. HEART RATE:

TODAY'S DISTANCE: WEATHER/TEMP:

TOTAL DISTANCE: MOOD ☺ 😐 ☹

WEEKLY SUMMARY & OBSERVATIONS:

SHORTEST RUN: LONGEST RUN: AVERAGE RUN:

WEEK TOTAL: MONTH TOTAL: YEAR TO DATE:

	M	T	W	TH	F	SA	SU
WEIGHT							
AM PULSE							
GLUCOSE							
KETONES BLOOD OR URINE							

MONTH: _____ WEEK OF: _____

GOALS: _____
_____

YOUR
FAVORITE
QUOTE
FOR THE WEEK:

MONDAY:

TIME: PACE: AVG. HEART RATE:

TODAY'S DISTANCE: WEATHER/TEMP:

TOTAL DISTANCE: MOOD ☺   ☹   ☹

TUESDAY:

TIME: PACE: AVG. HEART RATE:

TODAY'S DISTANCE: WEATHER/TEMP:

TOTAL DISTANCE: MOOD ☺   ☹   ☹

WEDNESDAY:

TIME: PACE: AVG. HEART RATE:

TODAY'S DISTANCE: WEATHER/TEMP:

TOTAL DISTANCE: MOOD ☺   ☹   ☹

THURSDAY:

TIME: PACE: AVG. HEART RATE:

TODAY'S DISTANCE: WEATHER/TEMP:

TOTAL DISTANCE: MOOD ☺   ☹   ☹

FRIDAY:

TIME: PACE: AVG. HEART RATE:

TODAY'S DISTANCE: WEATHER/TEMP:

TOTAL DISTANCE: MOOD ☺ 😐 ☹

SATURDAY:

TIME: PACE: AVG. HEART RATE:

TODAY'S DISTANCE: WEATHER/TEMP:

TOTAL DISTANCE: MOOD ☺ 😐 ☹

SUNDAY:

TIME: PACE: AVG. HEART RATE:

TODAY'S DISTANCE: WEATHER/TEMP:

TOTAL DISTANCE: MOOD ☺ 😐 ☹

WEEKLY SUMMARY & OBSERVATIONS:

SHORTEST RUN: LONGEST RUN: AVERAGE RUN:

WEEK TOTAL: MONTH TOTAL: YEAR TO DATE:

	M	T	W	TH	F	SA	SU
WEIGHT							
AM PULSE							
GLUCOSE							
KETONES BLOOD OR URINE							

MONTH: _____ WEEK OF: _____

GOALS: _____
_____

YOUR
FAVORITE
QUOTE
FOR THE WEEK:

MONDAY:

TIME: PACE: AVG. HEART RATE:

TODAY'S DISTANCE: WEATHER/TEMP:

TOTAL DISTANCE: MOOD ☺ 😐 ☹

TUESDAY:

TIME: PACE: AVG. HEART RATE:

TODAY'S DISTANCE: WEATHER/TEMP:

TOTAL DISTANCE: MOOD ☺ 😐 ☹

WEDNESDAY:

TIME: PACE: AVG. HEART RATE:

TODAY'S DISTANCE: WEATHER/TEMP:

TOTAL DISTANCE: MOOD ☺ 😐 ☹

THURSDAY:

TIME: PACE: AVG. HEART RATE:

TODAY'S DISTANCE: WEATHER/TEMP:

TOTAL DISTANCE: MOOD ☺ 😐 ☹

FRIDAY:

TIME: PACE: AVG. HEART RATE:

TODAY'S DISTANCE: WEATHER/TEMP:

TOTAL DISTANCE: MOOD ☺   ☻   ☹

SATURDAY:

TIME: PACE: AVG. HEART RATE:

TODAY'S DISTANCE: WEATHER/TEMP:

TOTAL DISTANCE: MOOD ☺   ☻   ☹

SUNDAY:

TIME: PACE: AVG. HEART RATE:

TODAY'S DISTANCE: WEATHER/TEMP:

TOTAL DISTANCE: MOOD ☺   ☻   ☹

WEEKLY SUMMARY& OBSERVATIONS:

SHORTEST RUN: LONGEST RUN: AVERAGE RUN:

WEEK TOTAL: MONTH TOTAL: YEAR TO DATE:

	M	T	W	TH	F	SA	SU
WEIGHT							
AM PULSE							
GLUCOSE							
KETONES BLOOD OR URINE							

MONTH: _____ WEEK OF: _____

GOALS: _____
_____

YOUR
FAVORITE
QUOTE
FOR THE WEEK:

MONDAY:

TIME: PACE: AVG. HEART RATE:

TODAY'S DISTANCE: WEATHER/TEMP:

TOTAL DISTANCE: MOOD ☺   😐   ☹

TUESDAY:

TIME: PACE: AVG. HEART RATE:

TODAY'S DISTANCE: WEATHER/TEMP:

TOTAL DISTANCE: MOOD ☺   😐   ☹

WEDNESDAY:

TIME: PACE: AVG. HEART RATE:

TODAY'S DISTANCE: WEATHER/TEMP:

TOTAL DISTANCE: MOOD ☺   😐   ☹

THURSDAY:

TIME: PACE: AVG. HEART RATE:

TODAY'S DISTANCE: WEATHER/TEMP:

TOTAL DISTANCE: MOOD ☺   😐   ☹

FRIDAY:

TIME: PACE: AVG. HEART RATE:

TODAY'S DISTANCE: WEATHER/TEMP:

TOTAL DISTANCE: MOOD ☺   😐   ☹

SATURDAY:

TIME: PACE: AVG. HEART RATE:

TODAY'S DISTANCE: WEATHER/TEMP:

TOTAL DISTANCE: MOOD ☺   😐   ☹

SUNDAY:

TIME: PACE: AVG. HEART RATE:

TODAY'S DISTANCE: WEATHER/TEMP:

TOTAL DISTANCE: MOOD ☺   😐   ☹

WEEKLY SUMMARY & OBSERVATIONS:

SHORTEST RUN: LONGEST RUN: AVERAGE RUN:

WEEK TOTAL: MONTH TOTAL: YEAR TO DATE:

	M	T	W	TH	F	SA	SU
WEIGHT							
AM PULSE							
GLUCOSE							
KETONES BLOOD OR URINE							

MONTH OF:

MON	TUES	WED	THURS
LIFE IS MESSY PAIN IS TEMPORARY RUN YOUR ASS OFF AND EMBRACE LIFE			

NOTES:

YEAR OF:

FRI	SAT	SUN	MONTHLY MUST DO LIST

MONTHLY GOALS

AFFIRMATIONS:

MONTH: _____ WEEK OF: _____

GOALS: _____

_____

YOUR
FAVORITE
QUOTE
FOR THE WEEK:

MONDAY:

TIME: PACE: AVG. HEART RATE:

TODAY'S DISTANCE: WEATHER/TEMP:

TOTAL DISTANCE: MOOD ☺ 😐 ☹

TUESDAY:

TIME: PACE: AVG. HEART RATE:

TODAY'S DISTANCE: WEATHER/TEMP:

TOTAL DISTANCE: MOOD ☺ 😐 ☹

WEDNESDAY:

TIME: PACE: AVG. HEART RATE:

TODAY'S DISTANCE: WEATHER/TEMP:

TOTAL DISTANCE: MOOD ☺ 😐 ☹

THURSDAY:

TIME: PACE: AVG. HEART RATE:

TODAY'S DISTANCE: WEATHER/TEMP:

TOTAL DISTANCE: MOOD ☺ 😐 ☹

FRIDAY:

TIME: PACE: AVG. HEART RATE:

TODAY'S DISTANCE: WEATHER/TEMP:

TOTAL DISTANCE: MOOD ☺ ☺ ☹

SATURDAY:

TIME: PACE: AVG. HEART RATE:

TODAY'S DISTANCE: WEATHER/TEMP:

TOTAL DISTANCE: MOOD ☺ ☺ ☹

SUNDAY:

TIME: PACE: AVG. HEART RATE:

TODAY'S DISTANCE: WEATHER/TEMP:

TOTAL DISTANCE: MOOD ☺ ☺ ☹

WEEKLY SUMMARY & OBSERVATIONS:

SHORTEST RUN: LONGEST RUN: AVERAGE RUN:

WEEK TOTAL: MONTH TOTAL: YEAR TO DATE:

	M	T	W	TH	F	SA	SU
WEIGHT							
AM PULSE							
GLUCOSE							
KETONES BLOOD OR URINE							

MONTH: _____ WEEK OF: _____

GOALS: _____

_____

YOUR
FAVORITE
QUOTE
FOR THE WEEK:

MONDAY:		
TIME:	PACE:	AVG. HEART RATE:
TODAY'S DISTANCE:		WEATHER/TEMP:
TOTAL DISTANCE:		MOOD ☺ ☺ ☹

TUESDAY:		
TIME:	PACE:	AVG. HEART RATE:
TODAY'S DISTANCE:		WEATHER/TEMP:
TOTAL DISTANCE:		MOOD ☺ ☺ ☹

WEDNESDAY:		
TIME:	PACE:	AVG. HEART RATE:
TODAY'S DISTANCE:		WEATHER/TEMP:
TOTAL DISTANCE:		MOOD ☺ ☺ ☹

THURSDAY:		
TIME:	PACE:	AVG. HEART RATE:
TODAY'S DISTANCE:		WEATHER/TEMP:
TOTAL DISTANCE:		MOOD ☺ ☺ ☹

FRIDAY:

TIME: PACE: AVG. HEART RATE:

TODAY'S DISTANCE: WEATHER/TEMP:

TOTAL DISTANCE: MOOD ☺ 😐 ☹

SATURDAY:

TIME: PACE: AVG. HEART RATE:

TODAY'S DISTANCE: WEATHER/TEMP:

TOTAL DISTANCE: MOOD ☺ 😐 ☹

SUNDAY:

TIME: PACE: AVG. HEART RATE:

TODAY'S DISTANCE: WEATHER/TEMP:

TOTAL DISTANCE: MOOD ☺ 😐 ☹

WEEKLY SUMMARY & OBSERVATIONS:

SHORTEST RUN: LONGEST RUN: AVERAGE RUN:

WEEK TOTAL: MONTH TOTAL: YEAR TO DATE:

	M	T	W	TH	F	SA	SU
WEIGHT							
AM PULSE							
GLUCOSE							
KETONES BLOOD OR URINE							

MONTH: _____ WEEK OF: _____

GOALS: _____

_____

YOUR
FAVORITE
QUOTE
FOR THE WEEK:

MONDAY:

TIME: PACE: AVG. HEART RATE:

TODAY'S DISTANCE: WEATHER/TEMP:

TOTAL DISTANCE: MOOD ☺ ☺ ☹

TUESDAY:

TIME: PACE: AVG. HEART RATE:

TODAY'S DISTANCE: WEATHER/TEMP:

TOTAL DISTANCE: MOOD ☺ ☺ ☹

WEDNESDAY:

TIME: PACE: AVG. HEART RATE:

TODAY'S DISTANCE: WEATHER/TEMP:

TOTAL DISTANCE: MOOD ☺ ☺ ☹

THURSDAY:

TIME: PACE: AVG. HEART RATE:

TODAY'S DISTANCE: WEATHER/TEMP:

TOTAL DISTANCE: MOOD ☺ ☺ ☹

FRIDAY:

TIME: PACE: AVG. HEART RATE:

TODAY'S DISTANCE: WEATHER/TEMP:

TOTAL DISTANCE: MOOD ☺   😐   ☹

SATURDAY:

TIME: PACE: AVG. HEART RATE:

TODAY'S DISTANCE: WEATHER/TEMP:

TOTAL DISTANCE: MOOD ☺   😐   ☹

SUNDAY:

TIME: PACE: AVG. HEART RATE:

TODAY'S DISTANCE: WEATHER/TEMP:

TOTAL DISTANCE: MOOD ☺   😐   ☹

WEEKLY SUMMARY & OBSERVATIONS:

SHORTEST RUN: LONGEST RUN: AVERAGE RUN:

WEEK TOTAL: MONTH TOTAL: YEAR TO DATE:

	M	T	W	TH	F	SA	SU
WEIGHT							
AM PULSE							
GLUCOSE							
KETONES BLOOD OR URINE							

MONTH: _____ WEEK OF: _____

GOALS: _____

_____

YOUR
FAVORITE
QUOTE
FOR THE WEEK:

MONDAY:

TIME: PACE: AVG. HEART RATE:

TODAY'S DISTANCE: WEATHER/TEMP:

TOTAL DISTANCE: MOOD ☺ 😐 ☹

TUESDAY:

TIME: PACE: AVG. HEART RATE:

TODAY'S DISTANCE: WEATHER/TEMP:

TOTAL DISTANCE: MOOD ☺ 😐 ☹

WEDNESDAY:

TIME: PACE: AVG. HEART RATE:

TODAY'S DISTANCE: WEATHER/TEMP:

TOTAL DISTANCE: MOOD ☺ 😐 ☹

THURSDAY:

TIME: PACE: AVG. HEART RATE:

TODAY'S DISTANCE: WEATHER/TEMP:

TOTAL DISTANCE: MOOD ☺ 😐 ☹

FRIDAY:

TIME: PACE: AVG. HEART RATE:

TODAY'S DISTANCE: WEATHER/TEMP:

TOTAL DISTANCE: MOOD ☺ 😐 ☹

SATURDAY:

TIME: PACE: AVG. HEART RATE:

TODAY'S DISTANCE: WEATHER/TEMP:

TOTAL DISTANCE: MOOD ☺ 😐 ☹

SUNDAY:

TIME: PACE: AVG. HEART RATE:

TODAY'S DISTANCE: WEATHER/TEMP:

TOTAL DISTANCE: MOOD ☺ 😐 ☹

WEEKLY SUMMARY & OBSERVATIONS:

SHORTEST RUN: LONGEST RUN: AVERAGE RUN:

WEEK TOTAL: MONTH TOTAL: YEAR TO DATE:

	M	T	W	TH	F	SA	SU
WEIGHT							
AM PULSE							
GLUCOSE							
KETONES BLOOD OR URINE							

MONTH: _____ WEEK OF: _____

GOALS: _____

_____

YOUR
FAVORITE
QUOTE
FOR THE WEEK:

MONDAY:		
TIME:	PACE:	AVG. HEART RATE:
TODAY'S DISTANCE:		WEATHER/TEMP:
TOTAL DISTANCE:		MOOD ☺ ☺ ☹

TUESDAY:		
TIME:	PACE:	AVG. HEART RATE:
TODAY'S DISTANCE:		WEATHER/TEMP:
TOTAL DISTANCE:		MOOD ☺ ☺ ☹

WEDNESDAY:		
TIME:	PACE:	AVG. HEART RATE:
TODAY'S DISTANCE:		WEATHER/TEMP:
TOTAL DISTANCE:		MOOD ☺ ☺ ☹

THURSDAY:		
TIME:	PACE:	AVG. HEART RATE:
TODAY'S DISTANCE:		WEATHER/TEMP:
TOTAL DISTANCE:		MOOD ☺ ☺ ☹

FRIDAY:

TIME: PACE: AVG. HEART RATE:

TODAY'S DISTANCE: WEATHER/TEMP:

TOTAL DISTANCE: MOOD ☺   😐   ☹

SATURDAY:

TIME: PACE: AVG. HEART RATE:

TODAY'S DISTANCE: WEATHER/TEMP:

TOTAL DISTANCE: MOOD ☺   😐   ☹

SUNDAY:

TIME: PACE: AVG. HEART RATE:

TODAY'S DISTANCE: WEATHER/TEMP:

TOTAL DISTANCE: MOOD ☺   😐   ☹

WEEKLY SUMMARY & OBSERVATIONS:

SHORTEST RUN: LONGEST RUN: AVERAGE RUN:

WEEK TOTAL: MONTH TOTAL: YEAR TO DATE:

	M	T	W	TH	F	SA	SU
WEIGHT							
AM PULSE							
GLUCOSE							
KETONES BLOOD OR URINE							

MONTH OF:

MON	TUES	WED	THURS
EVERY STEP YOU TAKE MAKES YOU A SUPERSTAR!			

NOTES:

YEAR OF:

FRI	SAT	SUN	MONTHLY MUST DO LIST

MONTHLY GOALS

AFFIRMATIONS:

MONTH: _____ **WEEK OF:** _____

GOALS: _____
_____

YOUR
FAVORITE
QUOTE
FOR THE WEEK:

MONDAY:

TIME: PACE: AVG. HEART RATE:

TODAY'S DISTANCE: WEATHER/TEMP:

TOTAL DISTANCE: MOOD ☺ 😐 ☹

TUESDAY:

TIME: PACE: AVG. HEART RATE:

TODAY'S DISTANCE: WEATHER/TEMP:

TOTAL DISTANCE: MOOD ☺ 😐 ☹

WEDNESDAY:

TIME: PACE: AVG. HEART RATE:

TODAY'S DISTANCE: WEATHER/TEMP:

TOTAL DISTANCE: MOOD ☺ 😐 ☹

THURSDAY:

TIME: PACE: AVG. HEART RATE:

TODAY'S DISTANCE: WEATHER/TEMP:

TOTAL DISTANCE: MOOD ☺ 😐 ☹

FRIDAY:

TIME: PACE: AVG. HEART RATE:

TODAY'S DISTANCE: WEATHER/TEMP:

TOTAL DISTANCE: MOOD ☺ ☻ ☹

SATURDAY:

TIME: PACE: AVG. HEART RATE:

TODAY'S DISTANCE: WEATHER/TEMP:

TOTAL DISTANCE: MOOD ☺ ☻ ☹

SUNDAY:

TIME: PACE: AVG. HEART RATE:

TODAY'S DISTANCE: WEATHER/TEMP:

TOTAL DISTANCE: MOOD ☺ ☻ ☹

WEEKLY SUMMARY & OBSERVATIONS:

SHORTEST RUN: LONGEST RUN: AVERAGE RUN:

WEEK TOTAL: MONTH TOTAL: YEAR TO DATE:

	M	T	W	TH	F	SA	SU
WEIGHT							
AM PULSE							
GLUCOSE							
KETONES BLOOD OR URINE							

MONTH: _____   WEEK OF: _____

GOALS: _____
_____

YOUR
FAVORITE
QUOTE
FOR THE WEEK:

MONDAY:

TIME: PACE: AVG. HEART RATE:

TODAY'S DISTANCE: WEATHER/TEMP:

TOTAL DISTANCE: MOOD ☺   😐   ☹

TUESDAY:

TIME: PACE: AVG. HEART RATE:

TODAY'S DISTANCE: WEATHER/TEMP:

TOTAL DISTANCE: MOOD ☺   😐   ☹

WEDNESDAY:

TIME: PACE: AVG. HEART RATE:

TODAY'S DISTANCE: WEATHER/TEMP:

TOTAL DISTANCE: MOOD ☺   😐   ☹

THURSDAY:

TIME: PACE: AVG. HEART RATE:

TODAY'S DISTANCE: WEATHER/TEMP:

TOTAL DISTANCE: MOOD ☺   😐   ☹

FRIDAY:

TIME: PACE: AVG. HEART RATE:

TODAY'S DISTANCE: WEATHER/TEMP:

TOTAL DISTANCE: MOOD ☺ ☺ ☹

SATURDAY:

TIME: PACE: AVG. HEART RATE:

TODAY'S DISTANCE: WEATHER/TEMP:

TOTAL DISTANCE: MOOD ☺ ☺ ☹

SUNDAY:

TIME: PACE: AVG. HEART RATE:

TODAY'S DISTANCE: WEATHER/TEMP:

TOTAL DISTANCE: MOOD ☺ ☺ ☹

WEEKLY SUMMARY & OBSERVATIONS:

SHORTEST RUN: LONGEST RUN: AVERAGE RUN:

WEEK TOTAL: MONTH TOTAL: YEAR TO DATE:

	M	T	W	TH	F	SA	SU
WEIGHT							
AM PULSE							
GLUCOSE							
KETONES BLOOD OR URINE							

MONTH: _____ WEEK OF: _____

GOALS: _____
_____

YOUR
FAVORITE
QUOTE
FOR THE WEEK:

MONDAY:

TIME: PACE: AVG. HEART RATE:

TODAY'S DISTANCE: WEATHER/TEMP:

TOTAL DISTANCE: MOOD ☺ 😐 ☹

TUESDAY:

TIME: PACE: AVG. HEART RATE:

TODAY'S DISTANCE: WEATHER/TEMP:

TOTAL DISTANCE: MOOD ☺ 😐 ☹

WEDNESDAY:

TIME: PACE: AVG. HEART RATE:

TODAY'S DISTANCE: WEATHER/TEMP:

TOTAL DISTANCE: MOOD ☺ 😐 ☹

THURSDAY:

TIME: PACE: AVG. HEART RATE:

TODAY'S DISTANCE: WEATHER/TEMP:

TOTAL DISTANCE: MOOD ☺ 😐 ☹

FRIDAY:

TIME: PACE: AVG. HEART RATE:

TODAY'S DISTANCE: WEATHER/TEMP:

TOTAL DISTANCE: MOOD ☺ 😐 ☹

SATURDAY:

TIME: PACE: AVG. HEART RATE:

TODAY'S DISTANCE: WEATHER/TEMP:

TOTAL DISTANCE: MOOD ☺ 😐 ☹

SUNDAY:

TIME: PACE: AVG. HEART RATE:

TODAY'S DISTANCE: WEATHER/TEMP:

TOTAL DISTANCE: MOOD ☺ 😐 ☹

WEEKLY SUMMARY & OBSERVATIONS:

SHORTEST RUN: LONGEST RUN: AVERAGE RUN:

WEEK TOTAL: MONTH TOTAL: YEAR TO DATE:

	M	T	W	TH	F	SA	SU
WEIGHT							
AM PULSE							
GLUCOSE							
KETONES BLOOD OR URINE							

MONTH: _____ WEEK OF: _____

GOALS: _____
_____

YOUR
FAVORITE
QUOTE
FOR THE WEEK:

MONDAY:

TIME: PACE: AVG. HEART RATE:

TODAY'S DISTANCE: WEATHER/TEMP:

TOTAL DISTANCE: MOOD ☺ 😐 ☹

TUESDAY:

TIME: PACE: AVG. HEART RATE:

TODAY'S DISTANCE: WEATHER/TEMP:

TOTAL DISTANCE: MOOD ☺ 😐 ☹

WEDNESDAY:

TIME: PACE: AVG. HEART RATE:

TODAY'S DISTANCE: WEATHER/TEMP:

TOTAL DISTANCE: MOOD ☺ 😐 ☹

THURSDAY:

TIME: PACE: AVG. HEART RATE:

TODAY'S DISTANCE: WEATHER/TEMP:

TOTAL DISTANCE: MOOD ☺ 😐 ☹

FRIDAY:

TIME: PACE: AVG. HEART RATE:

TODAY'S DISTANCE: WEATHER/TEMP:

TOTAL DISTANCE: MOOD ☺   😐   ☹

SATURDAY:

TIME: PACE: AVG. HEART RATE:

TODAY'S DISTANCE: WEATHER/TEMP:

TOTAL DISTANCE: MOOD ☺   😐   ☹

SUNDAY:

TIME: PACE: AVG. HEART RATE:

TODAY'S DISTANCE: WEATHER/TEMP:

TOTAL DISTANCE: MOOD ☺   😐   ☹

WEEKLY SUMMARY & OBSERVATIONS:

SHORTEST RUN: LONGEST RUN: AVERAGE RUN:

WEEK TOTAL: MONTH TOTAL: YEAR TO DATE:

	M	T	W	TH	F	SA	SU
WEIGHT							
AM PULSE							
GLUCOSE							
KETONES BLOOD OR URINE							

MONTH OF:

MON	TUES	WED	THURS
HOME IS WHERE YOUR FEET LAND			

NOTES:

YEAR OF:

FRI	SAT	SUN	MONTHLY MUST DO LIST

MONTHLY GOALS

AFFIRMATIONS:

MONTH: _____ WEEK OF: _____

GOALS: _____
_____

YOUR
FAVORITE
QUOTE
FOR THE WEEK:

MONDAY:

TIME: PACE: AVG. HEART RATE:

TODAY'S DISTANCE: WEATHER/TEMP:

TOTAL DISTANCE: MOOD ☺ 😐 ☹

TUESDAY:

TIME: PACE: AVG. HEART RATE:

TODAY'S DISTANCE: WEATHER/TEMP:

TOTAL DISTANCE: MOOD ☺ 😐 ☹

WEDNESDAY:

TIME: PACE: AVG. HEART RATE:

TODAY'S DISTANCE: WEATHER/TEMP:

TOTAL DISTANCE: MOOD ☺ 😐 ☹

THURSDAY:

TIME: PACE: AVG. HEART RATE:

TODAY'S DISTANCE: WEATHER/TEMP:

TOTAL DISTANCE: MOOD ☺ 😐 ☹

FRIDAY:

TIME: PACE: AVG. HEART RATE:

TODAY'S DISTANCE: WEATHER/TEMP:

TOTAL DISTANCE: MOOD ☺ 😐 ☹

SATURDAY:

TIME: PACE: AVG. HEART RATE:

TODAY'S DISTANCE: WEATHER/TEMP:

TOTAL DISTANCE: MOOD ☺ 😐 ☹

SUNDAY:

TIME: PACE: AVG. HEART RATE:

TODAY'S DISTANCE: WEATHER/TEMP:

TOTAL DISTANCE: MOOD ☺ 😐 ☹

WEEKLY SUMMARY & OBSERVATIONS:

SHORTEST RUN: LONGEST RUN: AVERAGE RUN:

WEEK TOTAL: MONTH TOTAL: YEAR TO DATE:

	M	T	W	TH	F	SA	SU
WEIGHT							
AM PULSE							
GLUCOSE							
KETONES BLOOD OR URINE							

MONTH: _____   **WEEK OF:** _____

GOALS: _____

_____

YOUR
FAVORITE
QUOTE
FOR THE WEEK:

MONDAY:

TIME: PACE: AVG. HEART RATE:

TODAY'S DISTANCE: WEATHER/TEMP:

TOTAL DISTANCE: MOOD ☺ 😐 ☹

TUESDAY:

TIME: PACE: AVG. HEART RATE:

TODAY'S DISTANCE: WEATHER/TEMP:

TOTAL DISTANCE: MOOD ☺ 😐 ☹

WEDNESDAY:

TIME: PACE: AVG. HEART RATE:

TODAY'S DISTANCE: WEATHER/TEMP:

TOTAL DISTANCE: MOOD ☺ 😐 ☹

THURSDAY:

TIME: PACE: AVG. HEART RATE:

TODAY'S DISTANCE: WEATHER/TEMP:

TOTAL DISTANCE: MOOD ☺ 😐 ☹

FRIDAY:

TIME: PACE: AVG. HEART RATE:

TODAY'S DISTANCE: WEATHER/TEMP:

TOTAL DISTANCE: MOOD ☺   😐   ☹

SATURDAY:

TIME: PACE: AVG. HEART RATE:

TODAY'S DISTANCE: WEATHER/TEMP:

TOTAL DISTANCE: MOOD ☺   😐   ☹

SUNDAY:

TIME: PACE: AVG. HEART RATE:

TODAY'S DISTANCE: WEATHER/TEMP:

TOTAL DISTANCE: MOOD ☺   😐   ☹

WEEKLY SUMMARY & OBSERVATIONS:

SHORTEST RUN: LONGEST RUN: AVERAGE RUN:

WEEK TOTAL: MONTH TOTAL: YEAR TO DATE:

	M	T	W	TH	F	SA	SU
WEIGHT							
AM PULSE							
GLUCOSE							
KETONES BLOOD OR URINE							

MONTH: _____ **WEEK OF:** _____

GOALS: _____
_____

YOUR
FAVORITE
QUOTE
FOR THE WEEK:

MONDAY:

TIME: PACE: AVG. HEART RATE:

TODAY'S DISTANCE: WEATHER/TEMP:

TOTAL DISTANCE: MOOD ☺   😐   ☹

TUESDAY:

TIME: PACE: AVG. HEART RATE:

TODAY'S DISTANCE: WEATHER/TEMP:

TOTAL DISTANCE: MOOD ☺   😐   ☹

WEDNESDAY:

TIME: PACE: AVG. HEART RATE:

TODAY'S DISTANCE: WEATHER/TEMP:

TOTAL DISTANCE: MOOD ☺   😐   ☹

THURSDAY:

TIME: PACE: AVG. HEART RATE:

TODAY'S DISTANCE: WEATHER/TEMP:

TOTAL DISTANCE: MOOD ☺   😐   ☹

FRIDAY:

TIME: PACE: AVG. HEART RATE:

TODAY'S DISTANCE: WEATHER/TEMP:

TOTAL DISTANCE: MOOD ☺ 😐 ☹

SATURDAY:

TIME: PACE: AVG. HEART RATE:

TODAY'S DISTANCE: WEATHER/TEMP:

TOTAL DISTANCE: MOOD ☺ 😐 ☹

SUNDAY:

TIME: PACE: AVG. HEART RATE:

TODAY'S DISTANCE: WEATHER/TEMP:

TOTAL DISTANCE: MOOD ☺ 😐 ☹

WEEKLY SUMMARY & OBSERVATIONS:

SHORTEST RUN: LONGEST RUN: AVERAGE RUN:

WEEK TOTAL: MONTH TOTAL: YEAR TO DATE:

	M	T	W	TH	F	SA	SU
WEIGHT							
AM PULSE							
GLUCOSE							
KETONES BLOOD OR URINE							

MONTH: _____ **WEEK OF:** _____

GOALS: _____
_____

YOUR
FAVORITE
QUOTE
FOR THE WEEK:

MONDAY:

TIME: PACE: AVG. HEART RATE:

TODAY'S DISTANCE: WEATHER/TEMP:

TOTAL DISTANCE: MOOD ☺   😐   ☹

TUESDAY:

TIME: PACE: AVG. HEART RATE:

TODAY'S DISTANCE: WEATHER/TEMP:

TOTAL DISTANCE: MOOD ☺   😐   ☹

WEDNESDAY:

TIME: PACE: AVG. HEART RATE:

TODAY'S DISTANCE: WEATHER/TEMP:

TOTAL DISTANCE: MOOD ☺   😐   ☹

THURSDAY:

TIME: PACE: AVG. HEART RATE:

TODAY'S DISTANCE: WEATHER/TEMP:

TOTAL DISTANCE: MOOD ☺   😐   ☹

FRIDAY:

TIME: PACE: AVG. HEART RATE:

TODAY'S DISTANCE: WEATHER/TEMP:

TOTAL DISTANCE: MOOD ☺ 😐 ☹

SATURDAY:

TIME: PACE: AVG. HEART RATE:

TODAY'S DISTANCE: WEATHER/TEMP:

TOTAL DISTANCE: MOOD ☺ 😐 ☹

SUNDAY:

TIME: PACE: AVG. HEART RATE:

TODAY'S DISTANCE: WEATHER/TEMP:

TOTAL DISTANCE: MOOD ☺ 😐 ☹

WEEKLY SUMMARY & OBSERVATIONS:

SHORTEST RUN: LONGEST RUN: AVERAGE RUN:

WEEK TOTAL: MONTH TOTAL: YEAR TO DATE:

	M	T	W	TH	F	SA	SU
WEIGHT							
AM PULSE							
GLUCOSE							
KETONES BLOOD OR URINE							

MONTH: _____ **WEEK OF:** _____

GOALS: ....

....

YOUR
FAVORITE
QUOTE
FOR THE WEEK:

MONDAY:

TIME: PACE: AVG. HEART RATE:

TODAY'S DISTANCE: WEATHER/TEMP:

TOTAL DISTANCE: MOOD ☺ 😐 ☹

TUESDAY:

TIME: PACE: AVG. HEART RATE:

TODAY'S DISTANCE: WEATHER/TEMP:

TOTAL DISTANCE: MOOD ☺ 😐 ☹

WEDNESDAY:

TIME: PACE: AVG. HEART RATE:

TODAY'S DISTANCE: WEATHER/TEMP:

TOTAL DISTANCE: MOOD ☺ 😐 ☹

THURSDAY:

TIME: PACE: AVG. HEART RATE:

TODAY'S DISTANCE: WEATHER/TEMP:

TOTAL DISTANCE: MOOD ☺ 😐 ☹

FRIDAY:

TIME: PACE: AVG. HEART RATE:

TODAY'S DISTANCE: WEATHER/TEMP:

TOTAL DISTANCE: MOOD ☺ 😐 ☹

SATURDAY:

TIME: PACE: AVG. HEART RATE:

TODAY'S DISTANCE: WEATHER/TEMP:

TOTAL DISTANCE: MOOD ☺ 😐 ☹

SUNDAY:

TIME: PACE: AVG. HEART RATE:

TODAY'S DISTANCE: WEATHER/TEMP:

TOTAL DISTANCE: MOOD ☺ 😐 ☹

WEEKLY SUMMARY & OBSERVATIONS:

SHORTEST RUN: LONGEST RUN: AVERAGE RUN:

WEEK TOTAL: MONTH TOTAL: YEAR TO DATE:

	M	T	W	TH	F	SA	SU
WEIGHT							
AM PULSE							
GLUCOSE							
KETONES BLOOD OR URINE							

MONTH OF:

AT A GLANCE

MON	TUES	WED	THURS
LIVE TO RUN RUN TO LIVE GET UP AND GO!			

NOTES:

YEAR OF:

FRI	SAT	SUN	MONTHLY MUST DO LIST
			MONTHLY GOALS

AFFIRMATIONS:

MONTH: _____ WEEK OF: _____

GOALS: _____
_____

YOUR
FAVORITE
QUOTE
FOR THE WEEK:

MONDAY:

TIME: PACE: AVG. HEART RATE:

TODAY'S DISTANCE: WEATHER/TEMP:

TOTAL DISTANCE: MOOD ☺ 😐 ☹

TUESDAY:

TIME: PACE: AVG. HEART RATE:

TODAY'S DISTANCE: WEATHER/TEMP:

TOTAL DISTANCE: MOOD ☺ 😐 ☹

WEDNESDAY:

TIME: PACE: AVG. HEART RATE:

TODAY'S DISTANCE: WEATHER/TEMP:

TOTAL DISTANCE: MOOD ☺ 😐 ☹

THURSDAY:

TIME: PACE: AVG. HEART RATE:

TODAY'S DISTANCE: WEATHER/TEMP:

TOTAL DISTANCE: MOOD ☺ 😐 ☹

FRIDAY:

TIME: PACE: AVG. HEART RATE:

TODAY'S DISTANCE: WEATHER/TEMP:

TOTAL DISTANCE: MOOD ☺   😐   ☹

SATURDAY:

TIME: PACE: AVG. HEART RATE:

TODAY'S DISTANCE: WEATHER/TEMP:

TOTAL DISTANCE: MOOD ☺   😐   ☹

SUNDAY:

TIME: PACE: AVG. HEART RATE:

TODAY'S DISTANCE: WEATHER/TEMP:

TOTAL DISTANCE: MOOD ☺   😐   ☹

WEEKLY SUMMARY & OBSERVATIONS:

SHORTEST RUN: LONGEST RUN: AVERAGE RUN:

WEEK TOTAL: MONTH TOTAL: YEAR TO DATE:

	M	T	W	TH	F	SA	SU
WEIGHT							
AM PULSE							
GLUCOSE							
KETONES BLOOD OR URINE							

MONTH: _____ WEEK OF: _____

GOALS: _____

_____

YOUR
FAVORITE
QUOTE
FOR THE WEEK:

MONDAY:

TIME: PACE: AVG. HEART RATE:

TODAY'S DISTANCE: WEATHER/TEMP:

TOTAL DISTANCE: MOOD ☺ 😐 ☹

TUESDAY:

TIME: PACE: AVG. HEART RATE:

TODAY'S DISTANCE: WEATHER/TEMP:

TOTAL DISTANCE: MOOD ☺ 😐 ☹

WEDNESDAY:

TIME: PACE: AVG. HEART RATE:

TODAY'S DISTANCE: WEATHER/TEMP:

TOTAL DISTANCE: MOOD ☺ 😐 ☹

THURSDAY:

TIME: PACE: AVG. HEART RATE:

TODAY'S DISTANCE: WEATHER/TEMP:

TOTAL DISTANCE: MOOD ☺ 😐 ☹

FRIDAY:

TIME:　　　　　　PACE:　　　　　AVG. HEART RATE:

TODAY'S DISTANCE:　　　　　　WEATHER/TEMP:

TOTAL DISTANCE:　　　　　　　　　　　MOOD ☺ 😐 ☹

SATURDAY:

TIME:　　　　　　PACE:　　　　　AVG. HEART RATE:

TODAY'S DISTANCE:　　　　　　WEATHER/TEMP:

TOTAL DISTANCE:　　　　　　　　　　　MOOD ☺ 😐 ☹

SUNDAY:

TIME:　　　　　　PACE:　　　　　AVG. HEART RATE:

TODAY'S DISTANCE:　　　　　　WEATHER/TEMP:

TOTAL DISTANCE:　　　　　　　　　　　MOOD ☺ 😐 ☹

WEEKLY SUMMARY & OBSERVATIONS:

SHORTEST RUN:　　　　LONGEST RUN:　　　AVERAGE RUN:

WEEK TOTAL:　　　　MONTH TOTAL:　　　YEAR TO DATE:

	M	T	W	TH	F	SA	SU
WEIGHT							
AM PULSE							
GLUCOSE							
KETONES BLOOD OR URINE							

MONTH: _____ WEEK OF: _____

GOALS: ....

....

YOUR
FAVORITE
QUOTE
FOR THE WEEK:

MONDAY:

TIME: PACE: AVG. HEART RATE:

TODAY'S DISTANCE: WEATHER/TEMP:

TOTAL DISTANCE: MOOD ☺   😐   ☹

TUESDAY:

TIME: PACE: AVG. HEART RATE:

TODAY'S DISTANCE: WEATHER/TEMP:

TOTAL DISTANCE: MOOD ☺   😐   ☹

WEDNESDAY:

TIME: PACE: AVG. HEART RATE:

TODAY'S DISTANCE: WEATHER/TEMP:

TOTAL DISTANCE: MOOD ☺   😐   ☹

THURSDAY:

TIME: PACE: AVG. HEART RATE:

TODAY'S DISTANCE: WEATHER/TEMP:

TOTAL DISTANCE: MOOD ☺   😐   ☹

FRIDAY:

TIME: PACE: AVG. HEART RATE:

TODAY'S DISTANCE: WEATHER/TEMP:

TOTAL DISTANCE: MOOD ☺ ☺ ☹

SATURDAY:

TIME: PACE: AVG. HEART RATE:

TODAY'S DISTANCE: WEATHER/TEMP:

TOTAL DISTANCE: MOOD ☺ ☺ ☹

SUNDAY:

TIME: PACE: AVG. HEART RATE:

TODAY'S DISTANCE: WEATHER/TEMP:

TOTAL DISTANCE: MOOD ☺ ☺ ☹

WEEKLY SUMMARY & OBSERVATIONS:

SHORTEST RUN: LONGEST RUN: AVERAGE RUN:

WEEK TOTAL: MONTH TOTAL: YEAR TO DATE:

	M	T	W	TH	F	SA	SU
WEIGHT							
AM PULSE							
GLUCOSE							
KETONES BLOOD OR URINE							

MONTH: _____ WEEK OF: _____

GOALS: _____
_____

YOUR
FAVORITE
QUOTE
FOR THE WEEK:

MONDAY:		
TIME:	PACE:	AVG. HEART RATE:
TODAY'S DISTANCE:		WEATHER/TEMP:
TOTAL DISTANCE:		MOOD ☺ ☺ ☹

TUESDAY:		
TIME:	PACE:	AVG. HEART RATE:
TODAY'S DISTANCE:		WEATHER/TEMP:
TOTAL DISTANCE:		MOOD ☺ ☺ ☹

WEDNESDAY:		
TIME:	PACE:	AVG. HEART RATE:
TODAY'S DISTANCE:		WEATHER/TEMP:
TOTAL DISTANCE:		MOOD ☺ ☺ ☹

THURSDAY:		
TIME:	PACE:	AVG. HEART RATE:
TODAY'S DISTANCE:		WEATHER/TEMP:
TOTAL DISTANCE:		MOOD ☺ ☺ ☹

FRIDAY:

TIME: PACE: AVG. HEART RATE:

TODAY'S DISTANCE: WEATHER/TEMP:

TOTAL DISTANCE: MOOD ☺ 😐 ☹

SATURDAY:

TIME: PACE: AVG. HEART RATE:

TODAY'S DISTANCE: WEATHER/TEMP:

TOTAL DISTANCE: MOOD ☺ 😐 ☹

SUNDAY:

TIME: PACE: AVG. HEART RATE:

TODAY'S DISTANCE: WEATHER/TEMP:

TOTAL DISTANCE: MOOD ☺ 😐 ☹

WEEKLY SUMMARY & OBSERVATIONS:

SHORTEST RUN: LONGEST RUN: AVERAGE RUN:

WEEK TOTAL: MONTH TOTAL: YEAR TO DATE:

	M	T	W	TH	F	SA	SU
WEIGHT							
AM PULSE							
GLUCOSE							
KETONES BLOOD OR URINE							

MONTH OF:

MON	TUES	WED	THURS
PUT ONE FOOT IN FRONT OF THE OTHER AND EVENTUALLY YOU'LL GET THERE — KEVIN			

NOTES:

YEAR OF:

FRI	SAT	SUN	MONTHLY MUST DO LIST
			_____
			_____
			_____
			_____
			_____

MONTHLY GOALS

_____

_____

_____

_____

_____

_____

_____

AFFIRMATIONS:

MONTH: _____ WEEK OF: _____

GOALS: _____

_____

YOUR
FAVORITE
QUOTE
FOR THE WEEK:

MONDAY:

TIME: PACE: AVG. HEART RATE:

TODAY'S DISTANCE: WEATHER/TEMP:

TOTAL DISTANCE: MOOD ☺ 😐 ☹

TUESDAY:

TIME: PACE: AVG. HEART RATE:

TODAY'S DISTANCE: WEATHER/TEMP:

TOTAL DISTANCE: MOOD ☺ 😐 ☹

WEDNESDAY:

TIME: PACE: AVG. HEART RATE:

TODAY'S DISTANCE: WEATHER/TEMP:

TOTAL DISTANCE: MOOD ☺ 😐 ☹

THURSDAY:

TIME: PACE: AVG. HEART RATE:

TODAY'S DISTANCE: WEATHER/TEMP:

TOTAL DISTANCE: MOOD ☺ 😐 ☹

FRIDAY:

TIME: PACE: AVG. HEART RATE:

TODAY'S DISTANCE: WEATHER/TEMP:

TOTAL DISTANCE: MOOD ☺ 😐 ☹

SATURDAY:

TIME: PACE: AVG. HEART RATE:

TODAY'S DISTANCE: WEATHER/TEMP:

TOTAL DISTANCE: MOOD ☺ 😐 ☹

SUNDAY:

TIME: PACE: AVG. HEART RATE:

TODAY'S DISTANCE: WEATHER/TEMP:

TOTAL DISTANCE: MOOD ☺ 😐 ☹

WEEKLY SUMMARY & OBSERVATIONS:

SHORTEST RUN: LONGEST RUN: AVERAGE RUN:

WEEK TOTAL: MONTH TOTAL: YEAR TO DATE:

	M	T	W	TH	F	SA	SU
WEIGHT							
AM PULSE							
GLUCOSE							
KETONES BLOOD OR URINE							

MONTH: _____ WEEK OF: _____

GOALS: _____
_____

YOUR
FAVORITE
QUOTE
FOR THE WEEK:

MONDAY:

TIME: PACE: AVG. HEART RATE:

TODAY'S DISTANCE: WEATHER/TEMP:

TOTAL DISTANCE: MOOD ☺ 😐 ☹

TUESDAY:

TIME: PACE: AVG. HEART RATE:

TODAY'S DISTANCE: WEATHER/TEMP:

TOTAL DISTANCE: MOOD ☺ 😐 ☹

WEDNESDAY:

TIME: PACE: AVG. HEART RATE:

TODAY'S DISTANCE: WEATHER/TEMP:

TOTAL DISTANCE: MOOD ☺ 😐 ☹

THURSDAY:

TIME: PACE: AVG. HEART RATE:

TODAY'S DISTANCE: WEATHER/TEMP:

TOTAL DISTANCE: MOOD ☺ 😐 ☹

FRIDAY:

TIME: PACE: AVG. HEART RATE:

TODAY'S DISTANCE: WEATHER/TEMP:

TOTAL DISTANCE: MOOD ☺ 😐 ☹

SATURDAY:

TIME: PACE: AVG. HEART RATE:

TODAY'S DISTANCE: WEATHER/TEMP:

TOTAL DISTANCE: MOOD ☺ 😐 ☹

SUNDAY:

TIME: PACE: AVG. HEART RATE:

TODAY'S DISTANCE: WEATHER/TEMP:

TOTAL DISTANCE: MOOD ☺ 😐 ☹

WEEKLY SUMMARY & OBSERVATIONS:

SHORTEST RUN: LONGEST RUN: AVERAGE RUN:

WEEK TOTAL: MONTH TOTAL: YEAR TO DATE:

	M	T	W	TH	F	SA	SU
WEIGHT							
AM PULSE							
GLUCOSE							
KETONES BLOOD OR URINE							

MONTH: _____ WEEK OF: _____

GOALS: _____

_____

YOUR
FAVORITE
QUOTE
FOR THE WEEK:

MONDAY:		
TIME:	PACE:	AVG. HEART RATE:
TODAY'S DISTANCE:		WEATHER/TEMP:
TOTAL DISTANCE:		MOOD ☺ 😐 ☹

TUESDAY:		
TIME:	PACE:	AVG. HEART RATE:
TODAY'S DISTANCE:		WEATHER/TEMP:
TOTAL DISTANCE:		MOOD ☺ 😐 ☹

WEDNESDAY:		
TIME:	PACE:	AVG. HEART RATE:
TODAY'S DISTANCE:		WEATHER/TEMP:
TOTAL DISTANCE:		MOOD ☺ 😐 ☹

THURSDAY:		
TIME:	PACE:	AVG. HEART RATE:
TODAY'S DISTANCE:		WEATHER/TEMP:
TOTAL DISTANCE:		MOOD ☺ 😐 ☹

FRIDAY:

TIME: PACE: AVG. HEART RATE:

TODAY'S DISTANCE: WEATHER/TEMP:

TOTAL DISTANCE: MOOD ☺ ☺ ☹

SATURDAY:

TIME: PACE: AVG. HEART RATE:

TODAY'S DISTANCE: WEATHER/TEMP:

TOTAL DISTANCE: MOOD ☺ ☺ ☹

SUNDAY:

TIME: PACE: AVG. HEART RATE:

TODAY'S DISTANCE: WEATHER/TEMP:

TOTAL DISTANCE: MOOD ☺ ☺ ☹

WEEKLY SUMMARY & OBSERVATIONS:

SHORTEST RUN: LONGEST RUN: AVERAGE RUN:

WEEK TOTAL: MONTH TOTAL: YEAR TO DATE:

	M	T	W	TH	F	SA	SU
WEIGHT							
AM PULSE							
GLUCOSE							
KETONES BLOOD OR URINE							

MONTH: _____ **WEEK OF:** _____

GOALS: _____
_____

YOUR
FAVORITE
QUOTE
FOR THE WEEK:

MONDAY:

TIME: PACE: AVG. HEART RATE:

TODAY'S DISTANCE: WEATHER/TEMP:

TOTAL DISTANCE: MOOD ☺   😐   ☹

TUESDAY:

TIME: PACE: AVG. HEART RATE:

TODAY'S DISTANCE: WEATHER/TEMP:

TOTAL DISTANCE: MOOD ☺   😐   ☹

WEDNESDAY:

TIME: PACE: AVG. HEART RATE:

TODAY'S DISTANCE: WEATHER/TEMP:

TOTAL DISTANCE: MOOD ☺   😐   ☹

THURSDAY:

TIME: PACE: AVG. HEART RATE:

TODAY'S DISTANCE: WEATHER/TEMP:

TOTAL DISTANCE: MOOD ☺   😐   ☹

FRIDAY:

TIME: PACE: AVG. HEART RATE:

TODAY'S DISTANCE: WEATHER/TEMP:

TOTAL DISTANCE: MOOD ☺   😐   ☹

SATURDAY:

TIME: PACE: AVG. HEART RATE:

TODAY'S DISTANCE: WEATHER/TEMP:

TOTAL DISTANCE: MOOD ☺   😐   ☹

SUNDAY:

TIME: PACE: AVG. HEART RATE:

TODAY'S DISTANCE: WEATHER/TEMP:

TOTAL DISTANCE: MOOD ☺   😐   ☹

WEEKLY SUMMARY & OBSERVATIONS:

SHORTEST RUN: LONGEST RUN: AVERAGE RUN:

WEEK TOTAL: MONTH TOTAL: YEAR TO DATE:

	M	T	W	TH	F	SA	SU
WEIGHT							
AM PULSE							
GLUCOSE							
KETONES BLOOD OR URINE							

MONTH OF:

MON	TUES	WED	THURS
HOW DO YOU FINISH A RACE? ONE STEP AT A TIME!			

NOTES:

YEAR OF:

FRI	SAT	SUN	MONTHLY MUST DO LIST
			MONTHLY GOALS

AFFIRMATIONS:

MONTH: _____   WEEK OF: _____

GOALS: _____
       _____

YOUR
FAVORITE
QUOTE
FOR THE WEEK:

MONDAY:

TIME: PACE: AVG. HEART RATE:

TODAY'S DISTANCE: WEATHER/TEMP:

TOTAL DISTANCE: MOOD ☺ 😐 ☹

TUESDAY:

TIME: PACE: AVG. HEART RATE:

TODAY'S DISTANCE: WEATHER/TEMP:

TOTAL DISTANCE: MOOD ☺ 😐 ☹

WEDNESDAY:

TIME: PACE: AVG. HEART RATE:

TODAY'S DISTANCE: WEATHER/TEMP:

TOTAL DISTANCE: MOOD ☺ 😐 ☹

THURSDAY:

TIME: PACE: AVG. HEART RATE:

TODAY'S DISTANCE: WEATHER/TEMP:

TOTAL DISTANCE: MOOD ☺ 😐 ☹

FRIDAY:

TIME: PACE: AVG. HEART RATE:

TODAY'S DISTANCE: WEATHER/TEMP:

TOTAL DISTANCE: MOOD ☺ 😐 ☹

SATURDAY:

TIME: PACE: AVG. HEART RATE:

TODAY'S DISTANCE: WEATHER/TEMP:

TOTAL DISTANCE: MOOD ☺ 😐 ☹

SUNDAY:

TIME: PACE: AVG. HEART RATE:

TODAY'S DISTANCE: WEATHER/TEMP:

TOTAL DISTANCE: MOOD ☺ 😐 ☹

WEEKLY SUMMARY & OBSERVATIONS:

SHORTEST RUN: LONGEST RUN: AVERAGE RUN:

WEEK TOTAL: MONTH TOTAL: YEAR TO DATE:

	M	T	W	TH	F	SA	SU
WEIGHT							
AM PULSE							
GLUCOSE							
KETONES BLOOD OR URINE							

MONTH: _____ WEEK OF:_____

GOALS: _____
_____

YOUR
FAVORITE
QUOTE
FOR THE WEEK:

MONDAY:		
TIME:	PACE:	AVG. HEART RATE:
TODAY'S DISTANCE:		WEATHER/TEMP:
TOTAL DISTANCE:		MOOD ☺ ☺ ☹

TUESDAY:		
TIME:	PACE:	AVG. HEART RATE:
TODAY'S DISTANCE:		WEATHER/TEMP:
TOTAL DISTANCE:		MOOD ☺ ☺ ☹

WEDNESDAY:		
TIME:	PACE:	AVG. HEART RATE:
TODAY'S DISTANCE:		WEATHER/TEMP:
TOTAL DISTANCE:		MOOD ☺ ☺ ☹

THURSDAY:		
TIME:	PACE:	AVG. HEART RATE:
TODAY'S DISTANCE:		WEATHER/TEMP:
TOTAL DISTANCE:		MOOD ☺ ☺ ☹

FRIDAY:

TIME: PACE: AVG. HEART RATE:

TODAY'S DISTANCE: WEATHER/TEMP:

TOTAL DISTANCE: MOOD ☺ 😐 ☹

SATURDAY:

TIME: PACE: AVG. HEART RATE:

TODAY'S DISTANCE: WEATHER/TEMP:

TOTAL DISTANCE: MOOD ☺ 😐 ☹

SUNDAY:

TIME: PACE: AVG. HEART RATE:

TODAY'S DISTANCE: WEATHER/TEMP:

TOTAL DISTANCE: MOOD ☺ 😐 ☹

WEEKLY SUMMARY & OBSERVATIONS:

SHORTEST RUN: LONGEST RUN: AVERAGE RUN:

WEEK TOTAL: MONTH TOTAL: YEAR TO DATE:

	M	T	W	TH	F	SA	SU
WEIGHT							
AM PULSE							
GLUCOSE							
KETONES BLOOD OR URINE							

MONTH: _____   WEEK OF: _____

GOALS: _____

_____

YOUR
FAVORITE
QUOTE
FOR THE WEEK:

MONDAY:

TIME: PACE: AVG. HEART RATE:

TODAY'S DISTANCE: WEATHER/TEMP:

TOTAL DISTANCE: MOOD ☺   😐   ☹

TUESDAY:

TIME: PACE: AVG. HEART RATE:

TODAY'S DISTANCE: WEATHER/TEMP:

TOTAL DISTANCE: MOOD ☺   😐   ☹

WEDNESDAY:

TIME: PACE: AVG. HEART RATE:

TODAY'S DISTANCE: WEATHER/TEMP:

TOTAL DISTANCE: MOOD ☺   😐   ☹

THURSDAY:

TIME: PACE: AVG. HEART RATE:

TODAY'S DISTANCE: WEATHER/TEMP:

TOTAL DISTANCE: MOOD ☺   😐   ☹

FRIDAY:

TIME: PACE: AVG. HEART RATE:

TODAY'S DISTANCE: WEATHER/TEMP:

TOTAL DISTANCE: MOOD ☺   😐   ☹

SATURDAY:

TIME: PACE: AVG. HEART RATE:

TODAY'S DISTANCE: WEATHER/TEMP:

TOTAL DISTANCE: MOOD ☺   😐   ☹

SUNDAY:

TIME: PACE: AVG. HEART RATE:

TODAY'S DISTANCE: WEATHER/TEMP:

TOTAL DISTANCE: MOOD ☺   😐   ☹

WEEKLY SUMMARY & OBSERVATIONS:

SHORTEST RUN: LONGEST RUN: AVERAGE RUN:

WEEK TOTAL: MONTH TOTAL: YEAR TO DATE:

	M	T	W	TH	F	SA	SU
WEIGHT							
AM PULSE							
GLUCOSE							
KETONES BLOOD OR URINE							

MONTH: _____   WEEK OF: _____

GOALS: _____

_____

YOUR
FAVORITE
QUOTE
FOR THE WEEK:

MONDAY:

TIME: PACE: AVG. HEART RATE:

TODAY'S DISTANCE: WEATHER/TEMP:

TOTAL DISTANCE: MOOD ☺   😐   ☹

TUESDAY:

TIME: PACE: AVG. HEART RATE:

TODAY'S DISTANCE: WEATHER/TEMP:

TOTAL DISTANCE: MOOD ☺   😐   ☹

WEDNESDAY:

TIME: PACE: AVG. HEART RATE:

TODAY'S DISTANCE: WEATHER/TEMP:

TOTAL DISTANCE: MOOD ☺   😐   ☹

THURSDAY:

TIME: PACE: AVG. HEART RATE:

TODAY'S DISTANCE: WEATHER/TEMP:

TOTAL DISTANCE: MOOD ☺   😐   ☹

FRIDAY:

TIME: PACE: AVG. HEART RATE:

TODAY'S DISTANCE: WEATHER/TEMP:

TOTAL DISTANCE: MOOD ☺   😐   ☹

SATURDAY:

TIME: PACE: AVG. HEART RATE:

TODAY'S DISTANCE: WEATHER/TEMP:

TOTAL DISTANCE: MOOD ☺   😐   ☹

SUNDAY:

TIME: PACE: AVG. HEART RATE:

TODAY'S DISTANCE: WEATHER/TEMP:

TOTAL DISTANCE: MOOD ☺   😐   ☹

WEEKLY SUMMARY & OBSERVATIONS:

SHORTEST RUN: LONGEST RUN: AVERAGE RUN:

WEEK TOTAL: MONTH TOTAL: YEAR TO DATE:

	M	T	W	TH	F	SA	SU
WEIGHT							
AM PULSE							
GLUCOSE							
KETONES BLOOD OR URINE							

MONTH OF:

MON	TUES	WED	THURS
RUN 'TILL YA PUKE!			

NOTES:

YEAR OF:

FRI	SAT	SUN	MONTHLY MUST DO LIST

MONTHLY GOALS

AFFIRMATIONS:

MONTH: _____ WEEK OF: _____

GOALS: _____

_____

YOUR
FAVORITE
QUOTE
FOR THE WEEK:

MONDAY:

TIME: PACE: AVG. HEART RATE:

TODAY'S DISTANCE: WEATHER/TEMP:

TOTAL DISTANCE: MOOD ☺ 😐 ☹

TUESDAY:

TIME: PACE: AVG. HEART RATE:

TODAY'S DISTANCE: WEATHER/TEMP:

TOTAL DISTANCE: MOOD ☺ 😐 ☹

WEDNESDAY:

TIME: PACE: AVG. HEART RATE:

TODAY'S DISTANCE: WEATHER/TEMP:

TOTAL DISTANCE: MOOD ☺ 😐 ☹

THURSDAY:

TIME: PACE: AVG. HEART RATE:

TODAY'S DISTANCE: WEATHER/TEMP:

TOTAL DISTANCE: MOOD ☺ 😐 ☹

FRIDAY:

TIME: PACE: AVG. HEART RATE:

TODAY'S DISTANCE: WEATHER/TEMP:

TOTAL DISTANCE: MOOD ☺   😐   ☹

SATURDAY:

TIME: PACE: AVG. HEART RATE:

TODAY'S DISTANCE: WEATHER/TEMP:

TOTAL DISTANCE: MOOD ☺   😐   ☹

SUNDAY:

TIME: PACE: AVG. HEART RATE:

TODAY'S DISTANCE: WEATHER/TEMP:

TOTAL DISTANCE: MOOD ☺   😐   ☹

WEEKLY SUMMARY & OBSERVATIONS:

SHORTEST RUN: LONGEST RUN: AVERAGE RUN:

WEEK TOTAL: MONTH TOTAL: YEAR TO DATE:

	M	T	W	TH	F	SA	SU
WEIGHT							
AM PULSE							
GLUCOSE							
KETONES BLOOD OR URINE							

MONTH: _____ WEEK OF: _____

GOALS: _____
_____

YOUR
FAVORITE
QUOTE
FOR THE WEEK:

MONDAY:		
TIME:	PACE:	AVG. HEART RATE:
TODAY'S DISTANCE:		WEATHER/TEMP:
TOTAL DISTANCE:		MOOD ☺ 😐 ☹

TUESDAY:		
TIME:	PACE:	AVG. HEART RATE:
TODAY'S DISTANCE:		WEATHER/TEMP:
TOTAL DISTANCE:		MOOD ☺ 😐 ☹

WEDNESDAY:		
TIME:	PACE:	AVG. HEART RATE:
TODAY'S DISTANCE:		WEATHER/TEMP:
TOTAL DISTANCE:		MOOD ☺ 😐 ☹

THURSDAY:		
TIME:	PACE:	AVG. HEART RATE:
TODAY'S DISTANCE:		WEATHER/TEMP:
TOTAL DISTANCE:		MOOD ☺ 😐 ☹

FRIDAY:

TIME: PACE: AVG. HEART RATE:

TODAY'S DISTANCE: WEATHER/TEMP:

TOTAL DISTANCE: MOOD ☺ ☺ ☹

SATURDAY:

TIME: PACE: AVG. HEART RATE:

TODAY'S DISTANCE: WEATHER/TEMP:

TOTAL DISTANCE: MOOD ☺ ☺ ☹

SUNDAY:

TIME: PACE: AVG. HEART RATE:

TODAY'S DISTANCE: WEATHER/TEMP:

TOTAL DISTANCE: MOOD ☺ ☺ ☹

WEEKLY SUMMARY & OBSERVATIONS:

SHORTEST RUN: LONGEST RUN: AVERAGE RUN:

WEEK TOTAL: MONTH TOTAL: YEAR TO DATE:

	M	T	W	TH	F	SA	SU
WEIGHT							
AM PULSE							
GLUCOSE							
KETONES BLOOD OR URINE							

MONTH: _____ WEEK OF: _____

GOALS: ....

....

YOUR
FAVORITE
QUOTE
FOR THE WEEK:

MONDAY:

TIME: PACE: AVG. HEART RATE:

TODAY'S DISTANCE: WEATHER/TEMP:

TOTAL DISTANCE: MOOD ☺ 😐 ☹

TUESDAY:

TIME: PACE: AVG. HEART RATE:

TODAY'S DISTANCE: WEATHER/TEMP:

TOTAL DISTANCE: MOOD ☺ 😐 ☹

WEDNESDAY:

TIME: PACE: AVG. HEART RATE:

TODAY'S DISTANCE: WEATHER/TEMP:

TOTAL DISTANCE: MOOD ☺ 😐 ☹

THURSDAY:

TIME: PACE: AVG. HEART RATE:

TODAY'S DISTANCE: WEATHER/TEMP:

TOTAL DISTANCE: MOOD ☺ 😐 ☹

FRIDAY:

TIME: PACE: AVG. HEART RATE:

TODAY'S DISTANCE: WEATHER/TEMP:

TOTAL DISTANCE: MOOD ☺   😐   ☹

SATURDAY:

TIME: PACE: AVG. HEART RATE:

TODAY'S DISTANCE: WEATHER/TEMP:

TOTAL DISTANCE: MOOD ☺   😐   ☹

SUNDAY:

TIME: PACE: AVG. HEART RATE:

TODAY'S DISTANCE: WEATHER/TEMP:

TOTAL DISTANCE: MOOD ☺   😐   ☹

WEEKLY SUMMARY & OBSERVATIONS:

SHORTEST RUN: LONGEST RUN: AVERAGE RUN:

WEEK TOTAL: MONTH TOTAL: YEAR TO DATE:

	M	T	W	TH	F	SA	SU
WEIGHT							
AM PULSE							
GLUCOSE							
KETONES BLOOD OR URINE							

MONTH: _____ WEEK OF: _____

GOALS: _____
_____

YOUR
FAVORITE
QUOTE
FOR THE WEEK:

MONDAY:		
TIME:	PACE:	AVG. HEART RATE:
TODAY'S DISTANCE:		WEATHER/TEMP:
TOTAL DISTANCE:		MOOD ☺ ☺ ☹

TUESDAY:		
TIME:	PACE:	AVG. HEART RATE:
TODAY'S DISTANCE:		WEATHER/TEMP:
TOTAL DISTANCE:		MOOD ☺ ☺ ☹

WEDNESDAY:		
TIME:	PACE:	AVG. HEART RATE:
TODAY'S DISTANCE:		WEATHER/TEMP:
TOTAL DISTANCE:		MOOD ☺ ☺ ☹

THURSDAY:		
TIME:	PACE:	AVG. HEART RATE:
TODAY'S DISTANCE:		WEATHER/TEMP:
TOTAL DISTANCE:		MOOD ☺ ☺ ☹

FRIDAY:

TIME: PACE: AVG. HEART RATE:

TODAY'S DISTANCE: WEATHER/TEMP:

TOTAL DISTANCE: MOOD ☺   😐   ☹

SATURDAY:

TIME: PACE: AVG. HEART RATE:

TODAY'S DISTANCE: WEATHER/TEMP:

TOTAL DISTANCE: MOOD ☺   😐   ☹

SUNDAY:

TIME: PACE: AVG. HEART RATE:

TODAY'S DISTANCE: WEATHER/TEMP:

TOTAL DISTANCE: MOOD ☺   😐   ☹

WEEKLY SUMMARY & OBSERVATIONS:

SHORTEST RUN: LONGEST RUN: AVERAGE RUN:

WEEK TOTAL: MONTH TOTAL: YEAR TO DATE:

	M	T	W	TH	F	SA	SU
WEIGHT							
AM PULSE							
GLUCOSE							
KETONES BLOOD OR URINE							

MONTH OF:

AT A GLANCE

MON	TUES	WED	THURS
IF YOU'RE GOING SOMEWHERE YOU MIGHT AS WELL BE RUNNING!			

NOTES:

YEAR OF:

FRI	SAT	SUN	MONTHLY MUST DO LIST

MONTHLY GOALS

AFFIRMATIONS:

MONTH: _____ WEEK OF: _____

GOALS: _____
_____

YOUR
FAVORITE
QUOTE
FOR THE WEEK:

MONDAY:		
TIME:	PACE:	AVG. HEART RATE:
TODAY'S DISTANCE:		WEATHER/TEMP:
TOTAL DISTANCE:		MOOD ☺ 😐 ☹

TUESDAY:		
TIME:	PACE:	AVG. HEART RATE:
TODAY'S DISTANCE:		WEATHER/TEMP:
TOTAL DISTANCE:		MOOD ☺ 😐 ☹

WEDNESDAY:		
TIME:	PACE:	AVG. HEART RATE:
TODAY'S DISTANCE:		WEATHER/TEMP:
TOTAL DISTANCE:		MOOD ☺ 😐 ☹

THURSDAY:		
TIME:	PACE:	AVG. HEART RATE:
TODAY'S DISTANCE:		WEATHER/TEMP:
TOTAL DISTANCE:		MOOD ☺ 😐 ☹

FRIDAY:

TIME: PACE: AVG. HEART RATE:

TODAY'S DISTANCE: WEATHER/TEMP:

TOTAL DISTANCE: MOOD ☺ 😐 ☹

SATURDAY:

TIME: PACE: AVG. HEART RATE:

TODAY'S DISTANCE: WEATHER/TEMP:

TOTAL DISTANCE: MOOD ☺ 😐 ☹

SUNDAY:

TIME: PACE: AVG. HEART RATE:

TODAY'S DISTANCE: WEATHER/TEMP:

TOTAL DISTANCE: MOOD ☺ 😐 ☹

WEEKLY SUMMARY & OBSERVATIONS:

SHORTEST RUN: LONGEST RUN: AVERAGE RUN:

WEEK TOTAL: MONTH TOTAL: YEAR TO DATE:

	M	T	W	TH	F	SA	SU
WEIGHT							
AM PULSE							
GLUCOSE							
KETONES BLOOD OR URINE							

MONTH: _____ WEEK OF: _____

GOALS: _____
       _____

YOUR
FAVORITE
QUOTE
FOR THE WEEK:

MONDAY:

TIME: PACE: AVG. HEART RATE:

TODAY'S DISTANCE: WEATHER/TEMP:

TOTAL DISTANCE: MOOD ☺   😐   ☹

TUESDAY:

TIME: PACE: AVG. HEART RATE:

TODAY'S DISTANCE: WEATHER/TEMP:

TOTAL DISTANCE: MOOD ☺   😐   ☹

WEDNESDAY:

TIME: PACE: AVG. HEART RATE:

TODAY'S DISTANCE: WEATHER/TEMP:

TOTAL DISTANCE: MOOD ☺   😐   ☹

THURSDAY:

TIME: PACE: AVG. HEART RATE:

TODAY'S DISTANCE: WEATHER/TEMP:

TOTAL DISTANCE: MOOD ☺   😐   ☹

FRIDAY:

TIME: PACE: AVG. HEART RATE:

TODAY'S DISTANCE: WEATHER/TEMP:

TOTAL DISTANCE: MOOD ☺ 😐 ☹

SATURDAY:

TIME: PACE: AVG. HEART RATE:

TODAY'S DISTANCE: WEATHER/TEMP:

TOTAL DISTANCE: MOOD ☺ 😐 ☹

SUNDAY:

TIME: PACE: AVG. HEART RATE:

TODAY'S DISTANCE: WEATHER/TEMP:

TOTAL DISTANCE: MOOD ☺ 😐 ☹

WEEKLY SUMMARY & OBSERVATIONS:

SHORTEST RUN: LONGEST RUN: AVERAGE RUN:

WEEK TOTAL: MONTH TOTAL: YEAR TO DATE:

	M	T	W	TH	F	SA	SU
WEIGHT							
AM PULSE							
GLUCOSE							
KETONES BLOOD OR URINE							

MONTH: _____ WEEK OF: _____

GOALS: _____

_____

YOUR
FAVORITE
QUOTE
FOR THE WEEK:

MONDAY:		
TIME:	PACE:	AVG. HEART RATE:
TODAY'S DISTANCE:		WEATHER/TEMP:
TOTAL DISTANCE:		MOOD ☺ ☐ ☹

TUESDAY:		
TIME:	PACE:	AVG. HEART RATE:
TODAY'S DISTANCE:		WEATHER/TEMP:
TOTAL DISTANCE:		MOOD ☺ ☐ ☹

WEDNESDAY:		
TIME:	PACE:	AVG. HEART RATE:
TODAY'S DISTANCE:		WEATHER/TEMP:
TOTAL DISTANCE:		MOOD ☺ ☐ ☹

THURSDAY:		
TIME:	PACE:	AVG. HEART RATE:
TODAY'S DISTANCE:		WEATHER/TEMP:
TOTAL DISTANCE:		MOOD ☺ ☐ ☹

FRIDAY:

TIME: PACE: AVG. HEART RATE:

TODAY'S DISTANCE: WEATHER/TEMP:

TOTAL DISTANCE: MOOD ☺ 😐 ☹

SATURDAY:

TIME: PACE: AVG. HEART RATE:

TODAY'S DISTANCE: WEATHER/TEMP:

TOTAL DISTANCE: MOOD ☺ 😐 ☹

SUNDAY:

TIME: PACE: AVG. HEART RATE:

TODAY'S DISTANCE: WEATHER/TEMP:

TOTAL DISTANCE: MOOD ☺ 😐 ☹

WEEKLY SUMMARY & OBSERVATIONS:

SHORTEST RUN: LONGEST RUN: AVERAGE RUN:

WEEK TOTAL: MONTH TOTAL: YEAR TO DATE:

	M	T	W	TH	F	SA	SU
WEIGHT							
AM PULSE							
GLUCOSE							
KETONES BLOOD OR URINE							

MONTH: _____ WEEK OF: _____

GOALS: ....

....

YOUR
FAVORITE
QUOTE
FOR THE WEEK:

MONDAY:		
TIME:	PACE:	AVG. HEART RATE:
TODAY'S DISTANCE:		WEATHER/TEMP:
TOTAL DISTANCE:		MOOD ☺ 😐 ☹

TUESDAY:		
TIME:	PACE:	AVG. HEART RATE:
TODAY'S DISTANCE:		WEATHER/TEMP:
TOTAL DISTANCE:		MOOD ☺ 😐 ☹

WEDNESDAY:		
TIME:	PACE:	AVG. HEART RATE:
TODAY'S DISTANCE:		WEATHER/TEMP:
TOTAL DISTANCE:		MOOD ☺ 😐 ☹

THURSDAY:		
TIME:	PACE:	AVG. HEART RATE:
TODAY'S DISTANCE:		WEATHER/TEMP:
TOTAL DISTANCE:		MOOD ☺ 😐 ☹

FRIDAY:

TIME: PACE: AVG. HEART RATE:

TODAY'S DISTANCE: WEATHER/TEMP:

TOTAL DISTANCE: MOOD ☺ 😐 ☹

SATURDAY:

TIME: PACE: AVG. HEART RATE:

TODAY'S DISTANCE: WEATHER/TEMP:

TOTAL DISTANCE: MOOD ☺ 😐 ☹

SUNDAY:

TIME: PACE: AVG. HEART RATE:

TODAY'S DISTANCE: WEATHER/TEMP:

TOTAL DISTANCE: MOOD ☺ 😐 ☹

WEEKLY SUMMARY & OBSERVATIONS:

SHORTEST RUN: LONGEST RUN: AVERAGE RUN:

WEEK TOTAL: MONTH TOTAL: YEAR TO DATE:

	M	T	W	TH	F	SA	SU
WEIGHT							
AM PULSE							
GLUCOSE							
KETONES BLOOD OR URINE							

Made in the USA
Middletown, DE
04 January 2021

30670598R00087